REBECCA NURSE MONUMENT, DANVERS.

The Witches of Salem

by
Winfield S. Nevins

1994

A Platinum Press Book

This special reprint edition originally published
in 1892 is now republished by:

Longmeadow Press
201 High Ridge Road
Stamford, CT 06904

in association with

Platinum Press Inc.
311 Crossways Park Drive
Woodbury, NY 11797

ISBN 0-681-00603-X

0987654321

Printed in the USA

Library of Congress Cataloging-in-Publication Data

Nevins, Winfield S.
    [Witchcraft in Salem village in 1692]
    The Witches of Salem / by Winfield S. Nevins.
        p. cm.
    Originally published: Witchcraft in Salem village in 1692.
Salem, Mass. : Shore Pub. Co. ; Boston : Lee and Shepard, 1892.
    Includes bibliographical references and index.
    ISBN 0-681-00603-X
    1. Witchcraft — Massachusetts — Salem. I. Title.
BF1576.N5 1994
133.4'3'097445 — dc20   93-47926
                                                    CIP

Contents.

			PAGE
List of Illustrations,		. . . .	5
Preface,		. . . . . .	6
Chap.	I.	Salem previous to 1692, .	9
Chap.	II.	Early Witchcraft Cases,	22
Chap.	III.	Outbreak in Salem Village,	46
Chap.	IV.	Court and Places of Trial,	70
Chap.	V.	Martha and Giles Corey, .	97
Chap.	VI.	Story of Rebecca Nurse,	111
Chap.	VII.	Rev. George Burroughs, .	131
Chap.	VIII.	Bridget Bishop and the Jacobs Family, . .	148
Chap.	IX.	The Procters, Willard, Carrier and How, . .	168
Chap.	X.	Susanna Martin, Mary Easty and others, . . .	190
Chap.	XI.	Accused and Tried but not Executed, . . .	210
Chap.	XII.	A Review, . . .	235

Appendix.

A.	List of Persons Accused, . . .	254
B.	Removal of Attainders and Recompense, ...	256
C.	Gov. Phips' Explanatory Letter, .	257
D.	The Bury St. Edmunds Case, . .	260

LIST OF ILLUSTRATIONS.

Rebecca Nurse Monument, ... Frontispiece.
Old First Church, Salem, ... 13
Gov. Bradstreet House, Salem, ... 42
Parris House, Danvers, ... 47
Salem Village Church, ... 53
Gadge House, Danvers, ... 55
Corner of Judge Corwin House, ... 69
Chief Justice Stoughton, ... 71
Judge Samuel Sewall, ... 72
Cotton Mather, ... 72
Corwin or Roger Williams House, ... 75
Site of 1692 Court House, ... 78
Cotton Mather's Grave, Boston, ... 81
Giles Corey Mill, ... 97
Ann Putnam House, Danvers, ... 108
Rebecca Nurse House, Danvers, ... 112
Fac Simile Nurse Examination, ... 126-7
Sarah Houlten House, Danvers, ... 130
Gallows Hill, Salem, ... 144
Trask House, North Beverly, ... 152
Bishop House, North Beverly, ... 157
Beadle Tavern, Salem, ... 160
Jacobs Grave, Danvers, ... 164
Procter House, Peabody, ... 169
Nathaniel Felton House, ... 175
Site Beadle Tavern, Salem, ... 180
Thomas Fuller House, Middleton, ... 183
Thomas Haines House, ... 201
Mary Putnam House, Danvers, ... 205
Phillip English House, Salem, ... 215
John Putnam, 3d, House, Danvers, ... 220
Witch Pins, Salem Court, Danvers, ... 231
Joseph Putnam House, Danvers, ... 237

PREFACE.

M Y design in writing this book has been to tell the story of the witchcraft delusion of 1692 in such a way as to convey a faithful picture to the reader. In order to do this it seemed advisable to give some account of the settlement of Salem and the neighboring villages, and their growth from 1626 to 1692, that the reader might understand the character of the people who lived there during the period covered by this history. Following this, will be found a chapter descriptive of the court that tried the accused persons, and a brief summary of its several sittings. A chapter devoted to some account of earlier witchcraft cases, in this country and in Europe, seemed also advisable, that we might the better understand that witchcraft was not new to the world in 1692, and that " Salem Witchcraft," so-called, differed from other witchcraft only in the details.

In succeeding chapters I have dealt with each of the individuals tried and executed, according to the interest in the case or the fullness of the documentary records that have come down to us. In addition to these, such mention is made of other cases, where the accused were not executed, as the circumstances connected with them seemed to demand. No chronological order is observed in this portion of the work. The aim has been in giving the evidence, to quote the exact language so far as space would permit, otherwise it has been abridged with strict regard to conveying the true meaning of the witness.

I make no claim to originality of material. Possibly a few documents and a few facts of interest may here be brought within the range of the reading public for the first time. If my view of the witchcraft delusion of 1692 and the responsibility therefor, differs somewhat from that entertained by most of those writers, I believe it is the one now generally accepted among historical students, and the one which the judgment of the future will pronounce correct. The mistake which, it seems to me, the majority of the writers on this chapter of our history have made, is that they did not put themselves in the places of the men and women of 1692, but judged by the standard of the latter half of the nineteenth century. I have tried to avoid this. Whether I have succeeded, the verdict of the reader alone will tell.

I have not deemed it necessary to give my authority for statements made when that authority was the records of the trials now on file in the court house in Salem. In all other cases where important statements are made on the authority of others, the reference is given. In the case of certain publications, like Calef's "More Wonders," and Mather's "Wonders of the Invisible World," the reference is usually to some recent edition, because the early editions of these works are not always accessible.

CHAPTER I.

SALEM PREVIOUS TO 1692.

SALEM was settled by the Puritans. Its settlement was a natural result of the Reformation in England. The hardy men and women who first came to ancient Naumkeag, came, not so much because of unjust law and tyrannical rulers, as because they could not respect the enforced forms of worship then existing in that country. They preferred the toils and privations of the wilderness in the new world to the tyranny of the Established Church and its supporters in the old.

In religious matters those who came to Salem differed somewhat from those who established themselves at Plymouth. The former were not true separatists from the Church of England; they were dissenters from its corruptions, its intolerance, and its formula only. In the words of the ministers at Salem, to John and Samuel Browne in 1629, they separated "not from the Church of England, but from its corruptions." "We came away," said they, "from the com-

mon prayer and ceremonies in our native land;
in this place of liberty we cannot, we will not,
use them." On the other hand, the people who
settled at Plymouth were separatists.[1]

John Lyford and a few followers left the Plymouth colony a few years after the settlement
there, owing "to dissatisfaction with the extreme separation from the English Church."
They settled at or near Nantasket, but in 1625
removed to Cape Ann. There they sought to
establish a fishing and farming community.
Roger Conant joined the colony in the fall of
1625 and was made "governor." The affairs
were in an unsatisfactory state. Fishing and
farming had been unprofitable. During the
succeeding spring Conant explored the coast to
the mouth of Naumkeag river and concluded to
make a settlement at Naumkeag. As a result
of this movement a company was formed in
England known as "the Governor and Colony
of the Massachusetts Bay in New England."
The company chose John Endicott governor,
and he, with his wife and a few others, sailed
for the new world on June 20, 1628. They arrived in Salem harbor early in September. On
the 16th of April, following, about two hundred
persons, including sixty females and twenty-six
children, left England to join the colony.

"They took with them one hundred and

1 Old Naumkeag, 2.

forty head of cattle, besides food, arms, clothing, and tools. There were four ministers in
the company. Two of them — Francis Higginson and Samuel Skelton — were men of
more than ordinary ability, and they were des-
tined to play no unimportant part in the history
of the new world."[2]

In the letters from the home company to Mr.
Higginson, during the following year or two,
we find much paternal advice. "Noe idle
drone (is to) be permitted to live among us."
Justice is urged in this spirit: "Wee hartely
pray you to admit of all complaints that shall
be made to you, or any of you that are of the
councell, be the complaints never so meane, and
pass it not slightly over but seriously examine
the truth of the business."

In another letter: "Wee pray you to make
some good lawes for the punishment of swear-
ers, whereof it is to be feared too many are
adicted."

The suppression of intemperance is urged, by
endeavoring "though there bee much strong
water sent for sale, so to order it as that salva-
ges may not for our lucre sake bee induced to
excessive use, or rather abuse of it," and by
punishing those "who shall become drunck."
The company urges that, "noe tobacco bee
planted unless it bee some small quantitie for
mere necessitie and for phisick for preservacon

2 Old Naumkeag, 9.

of their healths, and that the same bee taken
privately by ancient men and none others."

The first step after the arrival of the ministers and this large band of men and women,
was to form a church. The Plymouth church
had been transplanted with the emigrants from
Holland, but the men at Salem brought no
church with them. They decided to found one
which should be independent of all others and
of all higher ecclesiastical bodies. A meeting
was held on July 20, 1629, "as a solemn day of
humiliation for choyce of pastor and teacher
for Salem." The meeting was opened with
prayer and preaching, after which the vote was
taken "by each one writing in a note the name
of his choice." *This was the origin of the use
of the ballot in this country.*[3] Skelton was thus
chosen pastor, and Higginson, teacher. Having
made choice of these, the sixth day of August
was designated for the completion of the
church organization. On that day deacons and
ruling elders were chosen. Thus was fully constituted the First Church at Salem, and the
"*first Protestant Church in America*, on the
principle of the independence of each religious
community." No liturgy was used; unneces-
sary ceremonies were rejected, and "the simplicity of Calvin was reduced to a still plainer
standard."[4]

3 Bancroft's Hist. U. S., Centenary ed., I., 271.
4 Old Naumkeag, 12.

The "confession of faith and covenant" adopted was a very brief document, but it "comprised in a condensed shape and surpassing simplicity " [5] all that was necessary to bind together as a church of God this little col-

FIRST CHURCH.

ony of earnest men and women. It read as follows :

"We covenant with the Lord, and one with another, and do bind ourselves in the presence of God, to walk together in all His ways, according as He is pleased to reveal Himself unto us, in His blessed word of truth."

5 Rev. C. W. Upham, Dedicatory Address.

John and Samuel Browne, although opposed to state censorship and rebelling against the intolerance and corruption of the Established Church, desired that the liturgy and common prayer be used, and attempted to set up a church founded on that idea. They were sent back to England on the ground that the safety of the colony would be endangered by any want of unity.

In the summer of 1629 the entire government of the colony was transferred to John Winthrop and eleven followers on condition that they go and reside in New England. It was ostensibly a commercial operation; but it was actually the first step toward the formation of a future powerful and independent commonwealth.[6] Winthrop and some seven hundred others arrived in Salem in June of the following year. Bancroft has aptly described them as " a community of believers, professing themselves to be fellow members of Christ ; not a school of philosophers, proclaiming universal toleration and inviting associates without regard to creed."[7] On arriving at Salem they found the people in destitute circumstances, suffering for want of food, clothing and shelter. Winthrop was not favorably impressed with the location of the colony and explored the coast in

6 Old Naumkeag, 18.
7 Bancroft's U. S., I., 279.

the vicinity of the Mystic river, finally settling
at Charlestown, whither he shortly moved the
seat of government. The territory comprised
in the town of Salem at that time was much
greater than at present, including all of the
present city and the towns of Beverly, Danvers,
Marblehead, Peabody, Wenham, Manchester,
and parts of Topsfield and Middleton.

In 1692, with all the original territory set off
save Danvers and Middleton, the population
numbered 1700. It is evident to one who stud-
ies the history of the people in Salem and vicinity in 1632 and in 1692 that a change had
taken place between those periods in the character and general intelligence of the inhabitants.[8]
Many of the early settlers were men of educa-
tion, and, for those times, broad and liberal views.
Endicott, Winthrop, Higginson, Skelton and Saltonstall, and others of their associates, were
men of more than common mould. Endicott,
perhaps, in the opinion of some, exhibited a
little intolerance or contempt when he cut the
red cross from the flag because it reminded him
of popery, but it was no such ignorant superstition as that which led to the witchcraft delusion. There were other acts which we should
now call bigoted, but which in those days were

8 G. H. Moore's "Final Notes," 1885, 76. C. W. Upham in
Hist. Magazine, Sept., 1869, 140. Unden's "New England The-
ocracy," Conant's Translation, 222. Palfray, Hist. New England, 4, 128.

not so considered. No such men as those I have mentioned lived in Essex county in 1692, and few in the colony. Corwin, Hathorne, Parris, Noyes, the Putnams and their associates, were men of limited parts. I do not mean to imply that these men were inferior to their predecessors *because* they believed in witchcraft. Everybody believed in it then. Endicott and Winthrop had both signed death warrants for persons convicted of the crime ; or at least had not stayed the executions of the condemned. The people generally lacked the educational advantages of their ancestors. True, there was a Harvard College, but what was that poor, infant institution, with its library limited in volumes and variety, to Oxford and Cambridge, whence came some of the early settlers. The people were more likely, in 1692, to be carried away by such a cry as that of witchcraft than in 1632. Increase and Cotton Mather, of Boston, it is true, were learned men ; so was Rev. Mr. Willard, but the advice of these men and other Boston ministers was ignored. Some ministers there were in Boston and Salem who believed in all the current superstitions of the age and who sought to educate the people to believe in them, rather than to enlighten their minds and explain away, by the light of intelligence, seemingly strange occurrences. The age may well be termed the dark age of New Eng-

land history. The early dreams of independence of old England were dissipated ; religion
had lost its strong hold on the people. The
minister's power and influence were waning.
He could not lead the people as formerly. The
local unanimity, says Palfray, had been dissolved.[9] Parties had been formed with antag-
onistic views of local and colonial matters. In
affairs of church there were dissenters. Certain men in the community would brook no
dissent from the views which it pleased them
to hold. They deemed themselves infallible,
and were intolerant of all who differed from
them. Puritan bigotry stalked abroad more
than in 1629. But it encountered more opposition, and, for a time, opposition only increased
the narrowness and the intolerance.

Bancroft says : " New England, like Canaan,
had been settled by fugitives. Like the Jews,
they had fled to a wilderness ; like the Jews,
they looked to Heaven for light to lead them
on ; like the Jews, they had no supreme ruler
but God; like the Jews, they had heathen for
their foes ; and they derived their legislation
from the Jewish code. But for the people of
New England, the days of Moses and Joshua
were past; for them there was no longer a
promised land — they were in possession.
Reason now insisted on bringing the adopted

9 Hist. New England, iv., 3.

laws to the proof, that it might hold fast only
to the good.   Skepticism began to appear.
The fear of sorcery and the evil power of the
invisible world had sprung alike from the letter
of the Mosaic law and from the wonder excited
by the mysteries of nature . . . . . .
The belief in witchcraft had fastened itself on
the elements of faith and come deeply branded
into the common mind.   The people did not
rally to the error, they accepted the superstition only because it had not yet been disen-
gaged from religion.   The same causes which
had given energy to the religious principle had
given weight to the minister.   In the settlement of New England, the temple, or, as it
was called, the meeting house, was the centre
round which the people gathered.   As the
church had successfully assumed the exclusive
possession of civil franchises, the ambition of
the ministers had been both excited and grati-
fied.   They were not only the counsellors by
an unwritten law, they were the authors of
state papers, often employed on embassies, and,
at home, speakers at elections and in town
meetings."[10]   These ministers, like Parris, and
Noyes, and Hale, at the close of the seventeenth century, were losing their power and
their prominence because some few enlightened
men and thinkers were beginning to doubt.

10 Hist. U. S., Centenary Ed., 246-7.

They could continue their influence only by building on error and superstition. Any man or woman who doubted was their enemy. That person's power and influence must be crushed or the ministerial control was lost.

Between the settlement of Salem by Roger Conant in 1626 and the witchcraft days of 1692, the intolerance of the Puritans had been strikingly manifested on more than one occasion. The Brownes had been sent back to England for differing from Endicott and the First Church people ; Endicott had cut the red cross from the flag because it reminded him of popery ; Roger Williams had been banished from the colony for preaching that men should be allowed freedom of conscience in religious matters.[9] Quakers had been hung in Boston, and Quaker women, half naked, dragged through the streets of Salem at the tail of a cart and whipped, for maintaining the doctrines of their sect.[10] All this by a people who, within half a century, had come to these shores to worship according to the dictates of conscience. So, also, Thomas Scrugg, a deputy and a judge of the local court, for sympathy with Ann Hutchinson's Antimonian views, was proscribed, dis-

9 It was not Salem that banished Williams, but the colonial court. Salem remained true to him to the last.

10 These Quaker women had previously gone through the streets naked, voluntarily, to illustrate the spiritual nakedness of the people.

armed and deprived of his public functions ;
William Alford, for sympathizing with Scrugg,
was censured and disarmed and left the colony ;
Richard Waterman, an intelligent, industrious
man and law-abiding citizen, for dissenting from
the severe policy of the leading men of the
colony, was imprisoned and then banished ; even
Townsend Bishop, in 1645, because he did not
promptly bring forward an infant for baptism,
was handed over for discipline, and he a deputy
and local magistrate.   Lady Deborah Moody,
because she doubted the necessity of infant
baptism, was compelled to leave the colony.
Even in a much later day, William Gray was
persecuted in Salem for (political) opinion's
sake, and driven from the city.

Sir Edmund Andros, appointed by James II,
in 1686, the first royal governor of New England, had been deposed in 1688 for acts of op-
pression.   For nearly three years the people of
Massachusetts Bay colony governed themselves
entirely independent of the king of England.
On the accession of William and Mary, Sir
William Phips was appointed governor, and
came over in the spring of 1692, bringing with
him the new charter.   Phips was not an educated man, nor was he a man of much experience in public affairs.   He had commanded one
successful military expedition and one unsuc-
cessful naval expedition.   His rise to prominence

had been due in a large measure to great wealth, secured by raising buried Spanish treasure in the West Indies.

With this sketch of the history of the settlement of Salem, the people who constituted that settlement and the growth of the town, we are now prepared to consider the great calamity which befell the community two centuries ago.

CHAPTER II.

THE EARLY WITCHCRAFT CASES.

BELIEF in witchcraft, demonology, spiritualism and kindred isms, under slightly
differing names and phases, is as old as
the history of mankind. We read very early in
our Bible: "Thou shalt not suffer a witch to live."[1]
We find other mention of witchcraft in the Holy
Book, and so on down through all the pages of
history to the very year 1892.[2] In the twelfth
century it was believed that a witch was a

[1] Exodus xx : 18.

[2] The *Kadkaz*, a leading Russian journal, gave an interesting account, in the early part of 1889, of a revolting case of
witchcraft superstition. An old peasant woman, living near
Sookoom, in Caucasus, was suspected of witchcraft. Beyond
the infirmities of age, and, perhaps, of ill temper, the unhappy
wretch was no doubt as innocent as the victims of our own
witch finders were. Her son died, and immediately the rumor
ran that she had slain him with the assistance of the Evil One,
whose co-operation she had claimed. The neighbors sat in
judgment over her and decided that she should be submitted
to the ordeal by fire — that is to say, she was to be burned and
tortured in the hope that she would confess her supposed
crime. The terror of the poor old woman deprived her of co-
herent speech. This was assumed to be a proof of her guilt.
She was seized and tied to a pole and burned to death. What
gives a still more fiendish aspect to this carnival of cruelty is
that her surviving son was among the most energetic of those

woman who had made a secret compact with the devil and received from him power to ride through the air when going to meetings of kindred spirits. In 1484, Pope Innocent VIII, issued a bull, ordering the arrest of persons suspected of witchcraft. In 1485, forty-one aged women were burned at the stake in Burlia for substantially the same thing as was alleged against the men and women of Essex county in 1692, and others in Massachusetts earlier than that. Some years later, forty-eight persons were condemned in Ravensburg, and a hundred in Piedmont. In Geneva, in 1515, five hundred persons are said to have been executed for witchcraft in twelve weeks.[3] England, that

who tortured his mother. The peasantry of this remote region are said to be generally amiable and affectionate, and it is only when their supernatural terrors are aroused that they seek their own safety in malignant manifestations of fanatic cruelty.

Some of the negroes of the South still believe in the reality of witchcraft. In the spring of 1890 a woman of the name of Jaycox, living in Georgia, attempted to bewitch Willis Mitchell. She dropped a toad before his door after having decorated it with a long strip of red flannel in which she had tied numerous knots and to which she had attached pieces of white sewing thread and a bundle of red flannel in which were a lot of roots and sewing needles. See Journal of American Folk Lore, Vol. III, 205, "The Plantation Negro as a Freeman," by Bruce, and "Negro Myths from the Georgia Coast," by C. C. Jones. See also Appendix London Spiritual Magazine for 1868 for a case that happened in London that year ; Notes and Queries, London, V, 143 (4th series) ; Morganshire Advertiser, Eng., for 1862.

Rev. C. B. Rice of Danvers, has wisely pointed out the distinction between "Biblical witchcraft," and the "legal witchcraft" of the 17th Century.

3 Pop. Hist. U. S. II, 451

boasted land of light, liberty and law, has been
cursed with the superstition. History records
that as far back as the reign of King John,
about the year 1200, persons were executed for
the so-called crime. It continued to be a rec-
ognized crime down to 1712 in England, and
1727 in Scotland. Executions are recorded in
Aberdeen in 1597, when twenty-four persons
were burned to death. In the same place, in
1617, twenty-seven women were burned at the
stake. Others were hanged or burned in Bark-
ing, in 1575; in Chelmsford, Abington and
Cambridge, in 1579; thirteen in St. Osith's, in
1582. Ninety were hanged in 1645, and one
hundred and twenty in 1661. The last execution for witchcraft in England was in 1712, and
in Scotland in 1727.[4] Sir Mathew Hale, one of
the ablest of English jurists, tried many of
these cases and firmly believed there was such a
thing as witchcraft. Dr. More, Sir Thomas
Brown, Boyle, Cranmer, Edward Fairfax, and
many other of England's wise men were believers. When, therefore, such men as these
believed in witchcraft, how could the people
who dwelt in the American wilderness in 1692
be expected to doubt ? Chief Justice Holt was
the only man of prominence on the English
bench who, down to that time, had doubted the
correctness of the extreme view of the delu-

4 Ibd. 453.

sion. He at least protected the rights of the accused, which is more than was done by the judges at the trials in Salem.

The result of a century and a half of prosecutions, trials and executions in England, was a crop of books and pamphlets on the subject, mostly written by clergymen who had been believers and prosecutors, or by jurists who would naturally defend themselves and their associates and their interpretation of the law. Some of these books found their way to America. Many of them were read, during the long winter evenings, before the roaring open fires, by the simple New England people. Children were undoubtedly allowed access to them, as to the Bible and the Pilgrim's Progress. Mr. Parris himself seems to have founded his knowledge of the delusion on " Discourses of the Damned Art of Witchcraft," written about 1600 by William Perkins. As late as 1765, Blackstone, the great expounder of English law, wrote : " To deny the possibility, nay, actual existence of witchcraft and sorcery, is at once flatly to contradict the revealed word of God in various passages both of the Old and New Testament ; and the thing itself is a truth to which every nation in the world hath, in its time, borne testimony either by example, seemingly well attested, or by prohibitory laws which at least suppose the possibility of commerce with evil spirits." [5]   Blackstone adds that "these acts continued in force until lately to the terror of all ancient females in the kingdom, and many poor wretches were sacrificed thereby to the prejudice of their neighbors, and their own illusions, not a few having, by some means or other, confessed the fact at the gallows." [6]   How accurately this last sentence describes the condition of affairs in Essex county in 1692, we shall see in the future pages of this history.

What was witchcraft? What did people mean by the term? These are questions which should be understood in studying the delusion in the seventeenth century. In early times, witchcraft evidently meant, in connection with the terms sorcery, conjurer, etc., almost any singular conduct on the part of a person, more especially if that person were an aged female. The crabbedness of old age or misfortune was evidently looked upon as witchcraft. People whom we now term common scolds, neighborhood gossips,— those who, in some unaccountable manner, know the inmost secrets of their neighbors, what they have done and what they contemplate to do in the future,— would have been, two or three centuries ago, accused of witchcraft, in all human probability. Witches were persons supposed to have formed a com-

5 Chitty's Blackstone IV, 42.   6 Ibd., 43.

pact with the devil to torment God's people, and sometimes to cause their death. The apparitions of these bewitched persons were supposed to go through the air, mostly at night and on broom-sticks or poles, to a place of meeting. Many of them were charged with having signed a book presented to them for signature by his satanic majesty. This book was said to contain a contract which bound those who signed it to do his bidding. Sometimes, as was believed, they took the forms of negroes, hogs, birds or cats when going to perform their supernatural deeds.

For the punishment of witchcraft, in whatever form it appeared, the nations of the earth, as we have already seen, fixed the penalty of death, usually without benefit of clergy. England by the statute of 33 Henry VIII, chap. 8, declared all witchcraft and sorcery to be felony without benefit of clergy. Later, by statute of Jas. I, chap. 12, it was enacted that all persons invoking any evil spirit, or consulting or covenanting with, entertaining, employing, feeding, or rewarding any evil spirit, etc., should be guilty of felony without benefit of clergy, and suffer death.[7] Under the colonial charter, laws for the government of the colony were adopted, among them one against witchcraft. It provided that, "if any man or woman be a witch

7 Ibd., 43.

(that is, hath or consulteth with a familiar spirit) they shall be put to death." [8] When the charter was taken away, in 1684, these laws were abrogated. Whether they were revived by the proclamation of Andros, on his becoming governor, that all colony laws not repugnant to the laws of England would be observed,[9] and whether the forcible removal of the governor a few years later terminated them again, have been open questions among historians and lawyers. The early witchcraft prosecutions in 1692 were undoubtedly brought under the statute of James. That some of the later ones were is certain. Most of the indictments closed in these words — which would have been the form, probably, under English law direct, or colonial law approved by the king — " against the peace of our sovereign Lord and Lady, the king and queen, their crown and dignity, and against the form of the statute in that case made and provided." [10] The indictments against Samuel Wardwell and Rebecca Eames, however, refer directly to the statutes of James I. They were among the last found. The closing words are as follows : " with the evil speritt the devill a covenant did make, wherein he promised to honor worship & believe the devill contrary to

8 Notes on the History of Witchcraft in Mass., 1883, Geo. H. Moore, 6.

9 Ibd., 7.   9 Gray, 517.   Mass. Hist. Coll., 2d series, VIII, 77.

10 Essex Court Records.

the statute of King James the first in that behalf made and provided."[11]   This would seem to
settle beyond controversy the question which
has been raised, as to what law these prosecutions were made under.   On June 15, 1692, that
General Court which had convened on the 8th
in obedience to the summons of Gov. Phips,
passed an act to the effect that all local laws
made by the late Governor and Council of Massachusetts Bay and by the late government of
New Plymouth, being not repugnant to the laws
of England, should be and continue in force
until Nov. 10.   At the adjourned session in October a general crimes bill was passed, the second section of which read : "If any man or
woman be a witch, that is hath or consulteth
with a familiar spirit, they shall be put to
death."[12]   This was substantially the language
of the old colonial law.   On the 14th of the
following December an act was passed " for the
more particular direction in the execution of
the law against witchcraft."   The wording was
substantially that of the statute of James.
The first section declares that any person who
shall " use, practice or exercise any invocation
or conjuration of any wicked spirit or shall con-
sult, covenant with, entertain, or employ, feed
or reward any evil or wicked spirit . . . .

11 Ibd.   12 Province Laws, I., 55.

or take up any dead man, woman or child, out of his, her or their grave, or any other place where the dead body resteth, or the skin, bone or any other part of any dead person, to be employed or used in any manner of witchcraft, sorcery, charm or enchantment whereby any person shall be killed, destroyed, wasted or consumed, pined or lamed in his or her body, shall suffer the pains of death." The second section provides that if any person attempt by sorcery to discover any hidden treasure, or restore stolen goods, or provoke unlawful love, or hurt any man or beast, though the same be not effected, he shall be imprisoned one year and once every quarter stand on the pillory in the shire town six hours with the offence written in capital letters on his breast.[13] For a second offence of this nature the punishment was death. Both of these acts were disallowed on Aug. 22, 1695, but they had full force and effect in the meantime.

It is a little uncertain just when the first case of witchcraft arose in New England. Hutchinson says it was in 1645 at Springfield, Mass., when several persons were afflicted, among them two of the minister's children, and that every effort was made to convict some one of bewitching them,[14] but in vain. It is not quite certain

13 Province Laws, I., 90.   14 Hist. Mass., II., 16.

that Hutchinson has not here confounded the Springfield case of 1651 with this date.

The first execution for witchcraft in the new world was at Charlestown, in 1648, the victim being Margaret Jones. She was accused of practicing witchcraft, tried, found guilty, and hanged. The records of her case, if ever there were any, have long since been destroyed. The best account of it, undoubtedly, is that found in the journals of Gov. Winthrop. He was not only governor of the colony at the time, but presided at the trial. He says the evidence against her was "that she was found to have such a malignant touch as many persons, men, women and children, whom she stroked or touched with any affection or displeasure or &c., were taken with deafness, or vomitting, or other violent pains or sickness." Her medicines, being aniseseed or other harmless things, yet had, he says, such extraordinary effect, and she used to tell such as would not make use of her physic that they would never be healed, and "accordingly their diseases and hurts continued with relapses against the ordinary course." Again, Winthrop says, " in the prison there was seen in her arms a little child which ran from her into another room and the officer following it, it vanished."[15] Such is the story told by the judge who tried the case. Can we doubt the correctness of his summary of the evidence? No man in the colony

15 Winthrop's Journal, II., 326.

stood higher than John Winthrop. Margaret Jones, from all we can learn of her, was something of a physician, an "irregular practicioner," perhaps—what would be called a "quack" in this age. Possibly she met with success sometimes where a "regular" had failed. As indicating the sentiments of the times, it is worthy of note that the governor, a man naturally of sterling common sense, relates in his journal, that, "same day and hour she was executed, there was a very great tempest at Connecticut which blew down many trees."[16]

Shortly after the execution of Margaret Jones, her husband endeavored to secure passage to Barbadoes in a vessel then lying in Boston harbor with a hundred and eighty tons of ballast and eighty horses on board. He was refused passage because he was the husband of a witch, and "it was immediately observed that the vessel began to roll as if it would turn over." This strange action was alleged to be caused by Jones. The magistrates, being notified, issued their warrant for his arrest. As the officer, going to serve the warrant, was crossing in the ferry, the vessel continued to roll. He remarked that he had that which would tame the vessel and keep it quiet, at the same time exhibiting the document. Instantly the vessel ceased to roll, after having been in motion twelve hours. Jones was arrested and thrown into prison, and the vessel

16 Ibd.

rolled no more.[17]   He was not executed, and I do not find that he was ever tried.

Mary Parsons, wife of Hugh Parsons of Springfield, in 1649, circulated a report that the widow Marshfield was guilty of witchcraft. The widow began an action against the Parsons woman before Mr. Pynchon, the local magistrate, on the ground of slander. Mrs. Parsons was found guilty and sentenced to pay a fine of £3 or be whipped twenty lashes.[18] In May, 1651, Mary Parsons was herself charged with witchcraft on Martha and Rebekah Moxon, children of the minister. She was tried before the General Court in Boston, on May 13, 1651, and acquitted. She was then charged with the murder of her own child, to which charge she pleaded guilty, and the court sentenced her to be hanged. A reprieve was granted on May 29, but whether it was made permanent, is not known. Hugh Parsons was tried in Boston on May 31, 1652, on a charge of witchcraft, and acquitted.[19] The particulars in these cases are

17 Everett's Anecdotes of Early Local History.
18 King's Hand Book of Springfield.
19 Mass. Colonial Records for May 13, 1651. Also, May 31, 1652. Drake says Mary Parsons died in prison, and that she had charged her husband with bewitching her. (Hist. of Boston, 322.) Palfrey thinks she was executed. (Hist. New England, IV., 96, note.) A writer in the Mercurius Publicus, a London newspaper, of Sept. 25, 1651, says: " Four in Springfield were detected, whereof one was executed for murder of her own child and was doubtless a witch, another is condemned, a third under trial, a fourth under suspicion." (Ibd.)

very meagre. It is hardly safe to say that any statement relative to the final disposition of them is true beyond question. As showing somewhat the state of the public mind at that time, it is related that on the same day that Parsons was tried, the General Court appointed a day of humiliation, in consideration, among other things, "of the extent to which satan prevails amongst us in respect of witchcraft."[20]

John Bradstreet of Rowley was tried in Ipswich on July 28, 1652, on a charge of "familiarity with the devil." The order of the court, subsequently pronounced, was that "John Bradstreet upon his presentation of the last court for suspicion of having familiarity with the devil, upon examination of the case they found he had told a lie, which was a second, being convicted once before. The court sets a fine of 20 s. or else to be whipped."[21]

The next case of which we have a record was that of Ann Hibbins of Boston, a widow, whose husband had died in 1654. Hibbins had been a prosperous trader, but during the later years of his life had met with reverses, and soon sickened and died. This double affliction is said to have made his widow crabbed and meddlesome. At all events, she had so much trouble with her neighbors that the church censured her. During

20 Mass. Colonial Records for May 13, 1651.
21 Essex Court Papers.

the closing weeks of 1655 she was accused of being a witch. We have no record of her trial. We do not know just what the form of the charge against her was, nor the nature of the evidence. The jury returned a verdict of guilty, but the judges would not receive it. The case, under the law of the times, went to the General Court for trial. Mrs. Hibbins was called to the bar and pleaded not guilty. The evidence which had been taken in court was read and the witnesses, being present, acknowledged it. The General Court thereupon adjudged the woman guilty. Gov. John Endicott pronounced sentence, and she was hanged.[22] Mr. Beach, a minister at Jamaica, wrote in a letter to Increase Mather that Mr. Norton once said that Ann Hibbins was hanged for "having more wit than her neighbors; that the principal evidence against her was that, once on a time, seeing two neighbors conversing on the street she remarked that they were talking about her, and so it proved."[23] One John Scottow, a selectman and otherwise a prominent citizen, testified somewhat in favor of Mrs. Hibbins, and the court compelled him to write a most humble apology for having appeared to say a word in favor of one accused.[22] It is a little singular in this case that while the woman was a sister of Deputy

22 Mass. Colonial Record, VI., pt. 1, 269; also, Witchcraft Papers, State House, Boston.

Governor Bellingham,[23] and he could undoubtedly have exerted sufficient influence to save her, ·nothing of the kind appears to have been done.

In 1659, John Godfrey, an Essex county man, was accused of witchcraft, and bound over to the higher court. As no further record of his case is to be found, it is presumed he was either not brought to trial or, if so, was acquitted. He sued two of the prosecutors and witnesses against him and recovered damages from them. Another item on a later court record indicates that Godfrey was before the court and fined for being drunk.

Ann Cole of Hartford, Conn., in 1662, was concerned with two people of the name of Greensmith, man and wife, in some sort of transaction which brought against them all a charge of witchcraft. John Whiting wrote to Increase Mather that she was " a person esteemed pious, behaving herself with a pleasant mixture of humility and faith under very heavy suffering.[24] She made a " confession " of some nature and used the names of the Greensmiths to their prejudice. The Greensmith woman confessed that a demon had had carnal knowledge of her with much seeming delight to herself.[25] She was executed, and two of the others

23 Poole's Introduction to Johnson's Wonder Working Providences. Note, cxxix.

24 Mass. Hist. Col., VIII., 466.

25 Hutchinson's Hist. Mass. Bay, II., 23.

condemned, but probably not hanged. It looks very much as if, beneath all this piety and humility exhibited by Ann Cole, there was some evil ; that her conduct was not always perfect, and that to cover up her responsibility for evil deeds she confessed to being a witch.

The next case in chronological order was that of Elizabeth Knapp of Groton, Mass., in 1671. I quote largely from Putnam's account, condensed from the record left by Rev. Samuel Willard.[26] Elizabeth. was at first subject to mental moods and violent physical actions. Strange, sudden shrieks, strange changes of countenance appeared ; followed by the exclamations : " O, my leg," which she would rub ; " O, my breast," and she would rub that. Afterwards came fits in which she would cry out, " money, money," offered her as inducements to yield obedience, and sometimes, " sin and misery," as threats of punishment for refusal to obey the wishes of her strange visitant. Subsequently she barked like a dog and bleated like a calf. Then she told Mr. Willard he " was a great rogue." Some voice replied " I am not satan, I am a pretty black boy, this is my pretty girl." She charged Willard himself and some others of his parish with being her tormentors. Elizabeth Knapp's case seems to call for little

26 Putnam's Witchcraft Explained, etc., 157; also Mass. Hist. Coll., VIII., 555.

comment. We may form our own opinions as to the disorder from which she suffered.

The first important Essex County case of witchcraft was that which occurred in the family of William Morse of Newbury, now Newbury-port, in 1679. The family consisted, besides the old gentleman himself, of his wife, about sixty-five years of age, and a grandson, John Stiles, twelve or fifteen years of age. To show the condition of affairs as it appeared to Morse, I quote from his testimony :

About midnight, the door being locked when we went to bed, we heard a great hog in the house grunt and make a great noise, as we thought willing to get out. and that we might not be disturbed in our sleep I arose to let him out, and I found a hog in the house and the door unlocked. The door was firmly locked when we went to bed. The night following. I had a great awl lying in the window, the which awl we saw fall down out of the chimney into the ashes by the fire. After this I bid the boy put the same awl into the cupboard, which we saw done and the door shut to. This same awl came presently down the chimney again in our sight, and I took it up myself. Again the same night we saw a little Indian basket that was in the loft before come down the chimney again. And I took the same basket and put a brick into it, and the basket with the brick was gone, and came down again the third time with the brick in it, and went up again the fourth time and came down again without the brick, and the brick came down again a little after. The next day in the afternoon, my thread four times taken away, and came down the chimney, again my awl and gimlet wanting, again my leather taken away, came down the chimney, again my nails, being in the cover of a firkin, taken away, came down the chimney. The next day, being Sabbath day, I saw many stones and sticks, and pieces of bricks come down the chimney. On Monday I saw the andiron leap into the pot, dance and leap out again, leap in and dance and leap out again and leap on a table and there abide, and my wife saw the andirons on the table. Also I saw the pot turn itself over and throw down all the water.

Morse continued for some time to relate such occurrences as these. He subsequently testified that Caleb Powell came in and said : " This boy is the occasion of your grief, for he hath done these things, and hath caused˘ his poor old grandmother to be counted a witch." Powell then told Morse that he had seen young Stiles do many of the things, and that if he would let him have the boy he should be free from trouble. He did let Powell have the lad Monday night, and had no more trouble until Friday night. Then the strange performances were renewed. The old man's cap was pulled off his head and "the cat throwed at him." They put the cat out and shut the doors and windows, and presently she walked in. After they went to bed the cat was " throwed at them five times," once wrapped in a red waistcoat. Such is the story told under oath by an old man, whom Rev. Mr. Hale said was " esteemed a sincere and understanding Christian by those who knew him." He and his wife, under all the solemnities of their oaths,—and an oath meant much in those days,—made these startling depositions. What shall we say of them ? Have the statements exaggerated the facts ? How can they be met ? how explained ? Do we believe these old people wilfully falsified ? Caleb Powell seems to have suspected the boy John of mischievously perpetrating the tricks on the old people. He thought he could put an end to them by removing the youth from their house; and he did. So long as John was away there were none of those strange occurrences. Powell was a sea-faring man, and when on land dwelt near the Morses. He was perhaps a trifle boastful of his powers, and told these simple, untravelled people what remarkable things he could do, among others that he could detect witchcraft. We should naturally expect, after Powell had demonstrated to Morse that his grandson was a mischievous scapegrace, that the grandfather would have taken the boy home and given him a sound thrashing, and then thanked the man who had exposed the imposture. But no; it was an age of religious bigotry and superstition. Morse at once turned upon Powell and charged him with practicing witchcraft. Complaint was made against him in the local court on Dec. 3, 1679. His examination took place on Dec. 8, and the court ordered Morse to give bonds to prosecute at the next term of court in Ipswich. The case was heard on March 30, 1680. The court ordered, that though it found no grounds for the procedure against Powell, "yet he had given such ground for suspicion of his so dealing that they could not acquit him, but that he deserved to bear his own share of costs of prosecution."

Complaint was then made against Mrs. Morse herself, and on May 20, 1680, she was tried and convicted. Gov. Bradstreet, on May 27, after lecture in the meeting-house in Boston, sentenced her to be hanged. He granted a reprieve on June 1, until the next session of the court, when the reprieve was still further extended. The House of Deputies protested, and urged execution. In 1681, however, the House voted to give her a new trial, the magistrates concurring in the vote. We next hear of Mrs. Morse at her home in Newbury, through a letter written by Rev. John Hale in 1699. The records do not inform us whether she was ever tried again or how she obtained her liberty. All we know is, that from all the testimony, she lived a Christian life the remainder of her days, and always denied that she was ever guilty of witchcraft. Gov. Bradstreet, who passed sentence on Mrs. Morse, subsequently lived in Salem, and his remains were buried in the old Charter street burying ground. In 1692, as in 1680, he dared to resist the clamors of a misguided people and judiciary, and an unlearned, superstitious populace. Had Gov. Phips possessed his intelligence and firmness the harvest of death on Witch Hill would not have formed a part of our early

GOV. BRADSTREET'S HOME, SALEM.

American history. It is noteworthy that in 1692 the witchcraft delusion did not reach old Newbury. Her people evidently learned a lesson from the Morse case which they did not soon forget.

One of the latest and most interesting of the ante-Salem Village cases was that in the Goodwin family in 1688. The daughter of a Mrs. Glover was laundress in the Goodwin household in Boston. John Goodwin had four children, aged respectively thirteen, eleven, seven and five. The eldest, a girl named Martha, accused the laundress of carrying away some of the family linen. Mrs. Glover is described by Hutchinson[27] and Calef[28] as a " wild Irish woman of bad character." She talked harshly, perhaps profanely, to the children. The girl Martha immediately fell into a fit. The other children soon followed her example. "They were struck dead at the sight of the assembly's chatechism, Cotton Mather's ' Milk for Babes,' and some other good books, but could read the Oxford Jests, Popish and Quaker books and the Common Prayer, without any difficulties. Sometimes they would be deaf, then dumb, then blind, and sometimes all these disorders together would come upon them. Their tongues would be drawn down their throats, then pulled out upon their chins. Their jaws, necks, shoulders,

27 Hist. Mass., II., 25.   28 Fowler's Ed., 357.

elbows, and all their joints would appear to be dislocated, and they would make the most piteous outcries of burnings, of being cut with knives, &c. The ministers of Boston and Charlestown kept a day of fasting and prayers at the troubled house, after which the youngest child made no more complaints." The magistrates then interposed, and the elder Glover woman was apprehended. Upon examination she would neither confess nor deny, and appeared disordered in her senses. Physicians declared her to be of sound mind, whereupon she was convicted, sentenced and executed. The eldest child went to live in the family of the minister. For some time she behaved properly, and then had fits for a short time. Hutchinson says that after this they " returned to their ordinary behavior, lived to adult age, made profession of religion, and the affliction they had been under they publicly declared to be one motive to it. One of them, I knew many years after. She had the character of a very virtuous woman, and never made any acknowledgement of fraud in the transaction."[29]

It should be distinctly understood that the Glover woman was not prosecuted because of her religion. That had nothing to do with it. This case has sometimes been connected with the Salem cases of 1692, but it had no connection with them, either directly or indirectly.

29 Hist. Mass., II., 25-26.   Mass. Hist. Coll., VIII., 367.

I have thus traced, all too briefly, perhaps, the more important witchcraft cases in New England previous to 1692. Enough has here been given I trust, to show that the outbreak in Salem Village was nothing phenomenal; that it did not differ from what had happened elsewhere, save in obtaining a firmer hold in the minds of the people, and in being fostered by certain ministers and prominent men more than in other places. A few strong, calm words from them in February, 1692, would have summarily allayed the excitement and put an end to the whole wretched business. But those words were not spoken, and the tragedy followed.

NOTE. Beside the cases in New England previous to 1692, there were prosecutions for witchcraft in several southern states subsequent to that time. Grace Sherwood was accused in Princess Ann County, Virginia, in 1696. A jury of women searched her for witch marks, and the "water ordeal" was tried. That is, the sheriff was ordered to take "all such convenient assistance of boats and men as shall be by him thought fit, to meet at John Harper's plantation in order to take said Grace and put her [into water] above man's depth, and try her how she swims therein, always having care of her life to preserve her from drowning, and as soon as she came out that he request as many antient and knowing women as possible he can to search carefully for all marks or spots about her body not usual on others, etc." These "antient women" reported that they discovered certain distinctive marks of the woman. She was committed for trial.

Persons were accused of witchcraft in South Carolina in 1709, tried and sentenced to be burned at the stake. Drake says they were roasted by fire but there is no evidence that they were burned to death. J. Prince, Salem Gazette, Nov. 6, 1891,

CHAPTER III.

THE OUTBREAK IN SALEM VILLAGE.

THE witchcraft delusion of 1692 undoubtedly had its inception in the home of Rev. Samuel Parris, pastor of the church in Salem Village. In his family were a daughter, Elizabeth, nine years of age; a niece, Abigail Williams, eleven years of age; and a servant, Tituba, half Indian, half negro. The tradition is that the two girls, with perhaps a few other children of the neighborhood, used, during the winter of 1691-2, to assemble in the minister's kitchen and practice tricks and incantations with Tituba. Among the other girls of the neighborhood, some of whom are believed to have been present at a portion of these performances, were Ann Putnam, twelve years of age, daughter of Sergt. Thomas Putnam; Mercy Lewis, seventeen years of age, maid in the family of Sergt. Putnam; Elizabeth Hubbard, seventeen years of age, a niece of the wife of Dr. Griggs, the village physician, and a servant in the family; and Sarah Churchill, aged twenty years, a servant

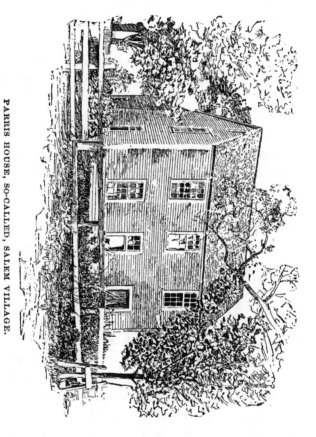

PARRIS HOUSE, SO-CALLED, SALEM VILLAGE.

[This building was added to the parsonage of 1692, after Parris departed.]

in the family of George Jacobs, Sen. Mercy Lewis had previously lived in the family of Rev. George Burroughs. During the winter these girls held occasional meetings in the neighborhood, usually at the minister's house. Calef says they began to act after a strange and unusual manner, by getting into holes and creeping under chairs and stools, and to use sundry odd postures and antic gestures, uttering foolish, ridiculous speeches, which neither they themselves nor any others could make sense of.[1]

This state of affairs continuing from late in December until into February, 1692, the elder people learned something of what was transpiring in their midst. Great was their consternation. Dr. Griggs was called, but as sometimes happens, even in this age of great learning, the doctor did not know what ailed the young people. Their "disease" was one unknown to medical science. Evidently feeling obliged to give some explanation of the disorder, the doctor declared that the girls were possessed of the devil, in other words, bewitched. Thereupon the curiosity of the whole community was awakened. People came from far and near to witness the strange antics of these children. Their credulity was taxed to its utmost. Mr. Parris, as was natural, was not only an interested spectator, but he took charge of the whole business.

1 Calef's More Wonders, Fowler's ed., 224.

He called a meeting of the ministers of the neighboring parishes to observe, to investigate, to pray. They came ; they saw ; they were conquered. They unanimously agreed with Dr. Griggs that the girls were bewitched. The all-important question was, Who or what caused them to act as they did ? Who bewitched them ? Whose spirit did the devil take to afflict them ? Mr. Parris and some of the ministers and prominent people of the village undertook to solve the mystery. Several private fasts were held at the minister's house, and several were held publicly. The children at first refused to tell anything about the mysterious affair. Tituba professed to know how to discover witches, and tried some experiments with that end in view. With the assistance of her husband, John Indian, she mixed some meal with urine of the afflicted and made a cake. The children, hearing that Tituba was attempting to discover the witches, are said to have "cried out" against her. They said she pinched, pricked and tormented them, and they fell into fits. She acknowledged that she had learned how to find out a witch, but denied that she was one herself. Tituba was called an Indian, but she was not a North American Indian. She and her husband, John, were brought from the West Indies by Mr. Parris when he came to Massachu-

setts Bay. They had been his slaves there.
Both spoke English but imperfectly and understood it only partially. In addition to Tituba,
the children named Sarah Good and Sarah Osburn as their tormentors. Most of the early
writers, think there was method in their mad-
ness. They describe Good as "a melancholy
distracted person," and Osburn as "a bed-ridden
old woman."[2] No one of the three women, they
reason, was likely to be believed in any denial
of the statements of these girls connected with
families of prominence and respectability.

This, in brief, is the story that has come down
to us from all the early and most of the later
writers. I am not disposed to deny its correctness ; but two or three suggestions occur in this
connection, which seem worthy of mention. Is
it probable that these girls, living miles apart, in
some instances five miles from the minister's
house, in a wilderness almost, where carriages
were unknown and bridle paths often dangerous,
would travel by night, in the dead of winter, to
Parris's house and home again ? Is it probable
that their parents or mistresses would allow
them out and away from home in this manner ?
Is it probable that such meetings, "circles" as
some call them, could be held at the minister's

house and he not know it, or knowing, would permit their continuance ?[3]

Tituba undoubtedly had familiarity with the strange tricks and jugglery practiced by the semi-barbarous races ; and, although we know nothing definite about it, is it not reasonable to presume that she exhibited some of these to Elizabeth Parris and Abigail Williams, who lived in the house with her, and that they told their young friends in the village about the performances ; that these friends came secretly to witness the mysterious tricks ; that they were instructed in the practice of them, and did practice them for self amusement or the amazement of other young people ; and that eventually the business got noised abroad and came to the knowledge of the elder people ? They would naturally institute an inquiry. The girls, probably, realized that if the exact truth were known to their elders they would be severely punished; possibly publicly disciplined in church. To prevent this, may they not have claimed that they could not help doing as they did ? They undoubtedly had some knowledge of witchcraft,

3 The writer knows of a case in a Salem school within recent years, where a girl of eight or ten years would throw herself full length on the floor, and roll and writhe, and pretend to be in the greatest agony. The teacher eventually discovered the imposture, but the girl continued her performances to the amazement and consternation of other school girls. When told by the teacher to " get up " she would do so promptly and go out to play.

enough at least to enable them to make a pretense of being bewitched. The girls could not for a moment realize the terrible consequences which were to follow. Having taken the first step, they were in the position of all who take a first step in falsehood or any other wrong doing, another step became necessary, and then another. Then they were probably commanded by their elders to tell who caused them to do these strange things ; or, as most writers put it, who "afflicted" them. As already stated, they named Tituba, Good and Osburn. Is it possible that we have misunderstood the first statements of these children ? Is it possible they did not say Tituba's *apparition caused* them to do certain strange things, but that they said *she taught* them ? Is it possible that Parris, to save scandal in his own immediate household, made Tituba declare that she had bewitched the girls? I do not mean to assert that this is the correct version of the outbreak of witchcraft in Salem Village. I only desire to suggest what may have been ; something which offers, perhaps, a rational explanation of the beginning of this horrid nightmare. Certainly such a course is as plausible, as reasonable, and has as much basis of fact as any of the theories heretofore advanced. We know nothing about these things as matter of absolute knowledge ; all is conjecture.

At all events, the children "named" the three
women as their tormentors. Joseph Hutchinson, Edward Putnam, Thomas Putnam and
Thomas Preston lodged complaint against Tituba, Good and Osburn ; and on Feb. 29, Jonathan

SALEM VILLAGE CHURCH, 1692.

Corwin and John Hathorne, the Salem magistrates, issued warrants for their arrest, the first
warrants issued for witchcraft in 1692. The examinations were begun on Tuesday, March 1,
1692. They were to have been held in the
house of Lieut. Nathaniel Ingersoll in Salem
Village, the tavern of the place; but the num-

bers who came to witness the opening scene in
this great drama of the new world could not be
accommodated in its rooms, and the court therefore adjourned to the meeting house.

As Sarah Good was the first person examined
I will deal with her case first. Sarah Good was
wife of William Good, "laborer." She is said
to have been about seventy years of age. Calef
says[4] she had long been counted a melancholy or
distracted woman; and Upham says[5] she was
broken down by wretchedness of condition and
ill-repute. Her answers to the questions propounded to her, as the reader will see, give no
evidence of coming from a person "broken
down," or "forlorn." She appears to have
answered with a fair degree of spirit. During
most of the first week in March, while on trial
before the local magistrates, Sarah Good was
taken to Ipswich jail every night and returned
in the morning, a distance of about ten miles
each way. From the testimony of her keepers
and the officers who escorted her to and from
jail, we learn that she exhibited considerable
animation. She leaped off her horse three times,
railed at the magistrates, and endeavored to kill
herself. Putnam says[6] there is no evidence that
Sarah Good ever had trouble with any of her
neighbors or accusers, or that any of them had

4 Fowler's Ed., 226.   5 Salem Witchcraft, II., 13.
6 Putnam's Witchcraft Explained, 334.

hostile feelings toward her. Evidently he had
never seen the testimony of the Abbeys and the
Gadges. Samuel Abbey, aged thirty-five, told
the magistrates that three years previous to the
hearing William and Sarah Good, being destitute
of a house, came to dwell in their house out of
charity ; that they let them live there until
Sarah Good was of " so turbulent a spirit, spite-

GADGE HOUSE, DANVERS.

ful and so maliciously bent " that they could not
suffer her to live in their house. Ever since
that time " Sarah Good hath carried it very
spitefully and malitiously towards them." After
she had gone from them they began to lose cattle, and lost several " in an unusual manner, in
a drooping condition, and yet they would eat."

Altogether they lost seventeen in two years, besides sheep and hogs; and " both doe believe they dyed of witchcraft." They further testified that William Good told them he went home one day and told his wife the Abbeys had lost two cows and she said she did not care if the Abbeys had lost all their cows. They concluded their testimony with this remarkable statement: " Just that very day that the said Sarah Good was taken up we the deponents had a cow that could not rise alone, but since presently after she was taken up, the said cow was well and could rise so well as if she had ailed nothing."

Sarah Gadge deposed that Sarah Good came to her house about two and a half years previously and wanted to come in; Gadge told her she could not, for she was afraid she had been with them that had had small pox, whereupon Good fell to muttering and scolding. The next morning Gadge's cows died, " in a sudden, terrible, and strange unusual manner soe that some of the neighbors said and deponent did think it to be done by witchcraft." The testimony of these witnesses shows that some of Good's accusers had had personal encounters with her, which may have engendered ill-feeling.

We come now to the examination of Sarah Good herself. It is given here as found on the court files in Salem. The warrant issued by Hathorne and Corwin charged her with " suspicion of witchcraft done to Elizabeth Parris,

Abigail Williams, Ann Putnam and Elizabeth Hubbard, at sundry times within this two months." This warrant was returned with the certificate of George Locker, constable, that he had "brought the person of the within named Sarah Good." Her testimony was written down by Ezekiel Cheever, and is given below. The examination was on the first and fifth. It is quite evident that only portions of the testimony were taken, and that is interspersed with comments by the reporter. And here a word of caution may as well be uttered, which will apply not more to the case of Sarah Good than to others. All the testimony in these trials, or examinations, before the local magistrates was taken by persons intensely prejudiced toward the prosecution. In reading it this should always be borne in mind. Much of it was taken by Parris himself. Knowing his feelings, and that he was the leading prosecutor very often, we feel that he would be pretty sure to devote more attention to testimony against the accused than to that in their favor. In fact, this is evidenced throughout the records which have been preserved.

The examination of Sarah Good before the Worshipful Esqrs. John Hathorne and Jonathan Corwin.

Sarah Good, what evil spirit have you familiarity with? —None.

Have you made no contracts with the devil?—No.

Why do you hurt these children?—I do not hurt them. I scorn it.

Who do you employ then to do it?—I employ nobody.

What creature do you employ then?—No creature: but I am falsely accused.

Why did you go away muttering from Mr. Parris's house? —I did not mutter, but thanked him for what he gave my child.

Have you no contract with the devil?—No.

Hathorne desired the children all of them to look upon her and see if this were the person that hurt them, and so they all did look upon her and said that this was one of the persons that did torment them. Presently they were all tormented.

Sarah Good, do you not see now what you have done? Why do you not tell us the truth? Why do you thus torment these poor children?—I do not torment them.

Who do you employ then?—I employ nobody. I scorn it.

How came they thus tormented?—What do I know? You bring others here and now you charge me with it.

Why who was it?—I do not know but it was some you brought into the meeting house with you.

We brought you into the meeting-house.—But you brought in two more.

Who is it then that tormented the children? It was Osburn.

What is it you say when you go muttering away from person's houses?—If I must tell I will tell.

Do tell us, then.—If I must tell, I will tell. It is the commandments: I may say my commandments, I hope.

What commandment is it?—If I must tell you, I will tell ; it is a psalm.

What psalm?

(After a long time she muttered over some part of a psalm.)

Who do you serve?—I serve God.

What God do you serve?—The God that made heaven

and earth (though she was not willing to mention the word " God "). Her answers were in a very wicked, spiteful manner, reflecting and retorting against the authority with base and abusive words; and many lies she was taken in. It was here said that her husband had said that she was either a witch or would be one very quickly. The worship-ful Mr. Hathorne asked him his reason why he said so of her, whether he had ever seen anything by her. He ans-wered: " No, not in this nature, but it was her bad carriage to him; and indeed," said he, " I may say with tears, that she is an enemy to all good."

Here is the account of this examination of Sarah Good as written down by Hathorne him-self:

Salem Village, March the first, 1692. Sarah Good, upon examination, denied the matter of fact, viz., that she ever used any witchcraft or hurt the above said children, or any of them. The above named children, being all present, positively accused her of hurting them sundry times within this two months, and also that morning. Sarah Good denied that she had been at their houses in said time or near them or had done them any hurt. All the above said children then present accused her face to face. Upon which they were all dreadfully tortured and tormented for a short space of time, and, the affliction and tortures, being over they charged said Sarah Good again that she had then so tortured them, and came to them and did it, although she was personally then kept at a considerable distance from them.

Sarah Good being asked if that she did not then hurt them, who did it, and the children being again tortured, she looked upon them, and said it was one of them we brought into the house with us. We asked her who it was. She then answered, and said it was Sarah Osburn, and Sarah Osburn was then under custody, and not in the house, and the children, being quickly after recovered out of their fit, said that it was Sarah Good and also Sarah Osburn that

then did hurt and torment or afflict them, although both of
them at the same time at a distance or remote from them
personally. There were also sundry other questions put to
her, and answers given thereunto by her according as is also
given in.

On March 7, Good, with Osburn and Tituba,
was sent to the jail in Boston. There she remained until June 28 when the grand jury presented an indictment against her as follows :

The jurors for our soverign Lord and Lady, the King
and Queen, present that Sarah Good, wife of William Good
of Salem Village, husbandman, the second day of May in
the fourth year of the reigne of our soverein Lord and
Lady, William and Mary, by the grace of God, of England,
Scotland, France and Ireland, King and Queen, defenders
of the faith &c., and divers other days and times, as well
before as after, certain detestable arts called witchcraft and
sorceries, wickedly and feloniously hath used, practiced
and exercised, at and within the township of Salem within
the county of Essex aforesaid, in upon and against one
Sarah Vibber, wife of John Vibber, of Salem aforesaid,
husbandman, by which said wicked arts she, said Sarah
Vibber, the said second day of May in the fourth year
abovesaid and divers other days and times as well before as
after, was and is afflicted, pined, consumed, wasted and
tormented, and also for sundry other acts of witchcraft by
said Sarah Good committed and done, before and since that
time, against the peace of our sovereign Lord and Lady,
the King and Queen, their crown and dignity and against
the forme of the statute in that case made and provided.

A second indictment charged her with practicing the same arts on Elizabeth Hubbard, a
third charged a similar offence committed on
Ann Putnam. The time alleged in the last two
indictments was March 1, which, it will be re-

membered, was the date of the preliminary examination. During the trial of these cases Deliverance Hobbs gave a " confession " as follows :

" Being at a meeting of the witches in Mr. Parris's field when Mr. Burroughs preached and administered the sacrament to them, saw Sarah Good among the rest and this fully agrees with what the afflicted relate."

Abigail Hobbs testified that she " was in company with Sarah Good and knows her to be a witch, and afterwards was taken deaf ; and Mary Walcott saw Good and Osburn run their fingers into this (deponent's) ears and a little after she spoke and said Good told her she should not speak." Mary Warren confessed that " Sarah Good is a witch and brought her the book to sign."

William Batten, William Shaw and Deborah Shaw testified that Susan Sheldon's hands were tied in such a manner that they were forced to cut the string. Sheldon told them it was Good Dustin that tied her hands ; that she had been thus tied four times in two weeks, " the two last times by Sarah Good." They further declared that whenever she touched the string she was bit ; also to a broom being carried out of the house and being put in a tree.

Johanna Chilburn testified that " the apparition of Sarah Good and her last child appeared to deponent and told her that its mother murdered it ; " that Good said she did it because she could not attend it; that the child told its mother she was a witch, and then "Sarah Good said she did give it to the devil."

Henry Herrick testified that Sarah Good came to his father's house and desired to lodge there; his father forbade it, and she went away grumbling. Being followed and forbidden to sleep in the barn, she replied that it would cost his father one or two of his best cows. Jonathan Batchelder added to this that about a week after two of his "master cattle" were removed and younger cattle put in their places, and since then several cattle had been let loose in a strange manner.

Elizabeth Hubbard, one of the afflicted, saw the apparition of Sarah Good, "who did most grieviously afflict her by pinching and pricking," and so continued hurting her until the first day of March, and then tortured her on that day, the day of her examination. She had also seen the apparition of Sarah Good afflict Elizabeth Parris, Abigail Williams, Ann Putnam and Sarah Vibber. "One night," she continued, "Samuel Sibley, that was attending me, struck Sarah Good on the arm." Susannah Sheldon said she had been most grievously tortured by the apparition of Sarah Good "biting, pricking, pinching and almost choking me to death." On June 26, 1692, Good most violently pulled her down behind a chest and tied her hands together with a wheel band and choked her, and William Battis and Thomas Buffinton were forced to cut the band from her hands, for they could not untie it. During the examination of Good this girl pretended to be afflicted, and said Sarah Good, by invisible hands, took a censer off the table and carried it out doors. Here is the deposition of Ann Putnam :

The deposition of Ann Putnam, Jr., who testifieth and saith that on the 25th of February, 1691-92, I saw the apparition of Sarah Good which did torture me most greviously, but I did not know her name until the 27th of February, and then she told me her name was Sarah Good. And then she did pinch me most greviously, and also since, several times urging me vehemently to write in her book. And also on the first of March, being the day of her examination, Sarah Good did most greviously torture me, and also several times since. And also on the first day of March, 1692, I saw the apparition of Sarah Good go and afflict the bodies of Elizabeth Parris, Abigail Williams and Elizabeth Hubbard. Also I have seen the apparition of Sarah Good afflicting the body of Sarah Vibber.   mark
                                        Ann x Putnam.

Sarah Vibber, a woman 36 years of age, testified that Good tortured Mercy Lewis on April 11, and herself on May 2, by pressing her breath almost out, and also afflicted her infant so that she and Vibber could not hold it. Since then the apparition of Sarah Good had pinched, beat and choked her, and pricked her with pins. Subsequently, one night, Good's apparition came into her room, pulled down the clothes and looked at her four years old child, and it had a great fit.

During this trial one of the witnesses who sat in the room cried out that Good had stabbed her, and had broken the knife-blade in so doing. The point of the blade was taken from her clothes where she said she was stabbed. Thereupon a young man arose in the court and stated that he broke that very knife the previous day and threw away the point. He produced the remaining part of the knife. It was then apparent that the girl had picked up the point which he threw away and put it in the bosom of her dress, whence she drew it to corroborate her statement that some one had stabbed her. She had deliberately falsified, and used the knife-point to reinforce the falsehood. If she was false in this statement, why not in all? If one girl falsified, how do we know whom to believe?

The most remarkable witness in this case, and in respect to age, the most remarkable in this whole history, was Dorcas Good. Dorcas was daughter of the accused Sarah Good, and only five years of age. She was called to testify against her own mother. Her evidence was merely that her mother "had three birds, one black, one yellow, and these birds hurt the children and afflicted persons." It may be as well to dispose of little Dorcas and her part in the witchcraft tragedy at this point as later. She was herself accused of being a witch, and three depositions against her are on the files.

"The deposition of Mercy Lewis, aged about nineteen years, who testefieth and saith that on the 2d of April, 1692, the apperishtion of Dorrithy Good, Sarah Good's daughter, came to me and did afflict me, urging me to write in her book and several times since Dorothy Good hath afflicted me, biting, pinching and choaking me, urging me to write in her book."

Mary Walcott deposed that March 21, " saw the apparition of Dorcas Good come to her, bit her, pinched her and afflicted her most grieviously, also almost choking her and urged her to write in a book." Ann Putnam testified to the same sort of torment in almost the exact words of Walcott. Dorcas was committed to jail with her mother. We have no further record of her. Whether she was ever tried is not known ; probably not. Certainly she was not executed.

Sarah Good was convicted and sentenced to be hanged. She was executed on July 19. Rev. Mr. Noyes, who was present, told her as she stood on the scaffold, " You are a witch, and you know you are a witch." " You are a liar," was her indignant reply; "I am no more a witch than you are a wizzard, and if you take my life, God will give you blood to drink."[7]

Sarah Osburn was about sixty years of age in 1692. Her husband was Alexander Osburn. Thirty years before, she had been married to Robert Prince, and still earlier to Thomas Small, both of whom were dead. Osburn came over

7 Calef, Fowler's Ed., 250.

from Ireland a few years previous to 1692, bound to service for a term of years to one of the settlers in the Village, in consideration of a sum of money advanced to pay his expenses to this country. The widow Prince, needing some one to manage her farm, bought out his unexpired time for fifteen pounds. He carried on the farm for a short time and then married the widow.[8] Their earlier life together and subse·quent marriage naturally gave rise to some gossip of an uncomplimentary nature. This, undoubtedly, was one of the inducements for the accusing girls to "cry out" against her among the first. The Osburns appear to have been in comfortable circumstances. Their greatest cross was the illness which confined the wife to her bed much of the time. Both were members of the church, and so far as we know, they were devout Christians, sober and industrious citizens.

Sarah Osburn was examined before the local magistrates on the first, second and third of March. No particularly new or interesting facts were developed. Her examination was very nearly a repetition of the proceedings in the case of Sarah Good. She denied having familiarity with any evil spirit, or having made any contract with the devil, and said she did not hurt the children or employ any one to hurt

8 Salem Witchcraft, II., 17.

them. " Mr. Hathorne," says Cheever's report,
" desired all the children to stand up and look
upon her, and see if they did not know her,
which they all did. And every one of them
said that this was one of the women᾿ that did
afflict them, and that they had constantly seen
her in the very habit she was now in. Three
evidences declared that she said this
morning that she was more like to be
bewitched than that she was a witch. Mr.
Hathorne asked what made her say so. She
answered that she was frightened one time in
her sleep, and either saw or dreamed she saw a
thing like an Indian, all black, which did pinch
her in the neck, and pulled her by the back part
of her head to the door of the house." The
woman was sent to jail in Boston. There she
died. The excitement and mental strain of the
arrest and examination, the exposure in going to
and from Ipswich jail, and the hardships of jail
life in Boston, together with the ill-treatment
and brutality to which all the accused were sub-
jected, proved fatal to this feeble old woman.
The last record in her case is this bill of the
Boston jailer : " To chains for Sarah Good and
Sarah Osburn, 14 shillings. To the keeping of
Sarah Osburn from the 7th March to 10 May,
when she died, being nine weeks and two days,
1£. 3s. 5d."⁹ In the fullest sense of the word,

9 Essex Court Records.

Sarah Osburn was one of the " victims " of the witchcraft delusion of 1692.

Tituba, in the course of her examination, told a rambling and somewhat disjointed story, evidently due partly to her want of comprehension of the English language, and the broken English in which she was obliged to reply. Asked if she ever went on a witch expedition with Good and Osburn, she replied ; " They are very strong and pull me, and make me go with them." " Where did you go," asked the magistrate. " Up to Mr. Putnam's and make me hurt the child." " Who did make you go ? " "A man that is very strong, and these two women, Good and Osburn, but I am sorry." " How did you go ? What do you ride upon?" " I ride upon a stick or pole, and Good and Osburn behind me ; we ride taking hold of one another ; I don't know how we go, for I saw no trees or path, but was presently there when we were up." She declared that she never practiced witchcraft in her own country. Asked what sights she saw when she went abroad, she replied : " I see a man, a dog, a hog, and two cats, a black and red, and the strange monster was Osburn's that I mentioned before, this was the hairy imp. The man would give it to me but I would not have it." To the jail in Boston went Tituba also. Calef says she was " afterwards committed to prison and lay there until sold for her fees." She declared

that her master beat her and otherwise abused
her to make her confess and accuse others of
witchcraft; that whatever she said by way of
accusing others was because of such treatment,
and that her master refused to pay her fees unless she would stand to her confession.[10]   Drake
says Tituba was sold to pay her prison fees after
lying there thirteen months.[11]   She was never
tried before any court.

10 Fowler's Ed., 227.   11 Annals of N. E., 190.

CORNER OF JUDGE CORWIN HOUSE.

CHAPTER IV.

THE COURT AND PLACES OF TRIAL.

HEN Gov. Phips arrived in Boston on May 14, 1692, he found the jails filled with persons accused of witchcraft. No courts existed; they had fallen with the " provisional government " which succeeded the Andros administration. The charter that Phips brought over empowered the General Court to erect and constitute judicatories and courts of record or other courts, of which the Governor was to appoint the judges.[1] No meeting of the General Court could be held until after an election of members, which must be two or three weeks later. Immediate trial of the accused was demanded as their right, and also to relieve the overcrowded condition of the jails. It had long been the custom in England, in cases of emergency, for the king to appoint Commissioners of Oyer and Terminer to hear and decide the causes.[2] In the absence of courts and as the

1 Province charter, 1692. Province Laws, I., 1.
2 Chitty's Blackstone, Book IV., 221.

personal representative of the King, no doubt,
Gov. Phips issued a commission for a court of
Oyer and Terminer.[3]   He appointed the commissioners on May 27.   William Stoughton, the
deputy governor, was named first and always
presided as chief justice. His previous political

CHIEF JUSTICE STOUGHTON.

affiliations had made him somewhat unpopular
with the people. As a candidate for a judicial
position under the preceding administration, he

3 " May 27, 1692. Upon consideration that there are many
criminal offenders now in custody some whereof have lyen long
and many inconveniences attending the thronging of the goals
at this hot season of the year, there being no judacatories or
courts of justices yet established." Preamble to order of
Council establishing the court. Ex. Recd., II., 176.

received not a single vote.[4] Stoughton was educated for the ministry and not the law, but all accounts agree that he was a very able man. He was not without judicial experience, for he sat with Dudley and others at the trial of Mary Glover in 1688. Stoughton was a great friend of the Mathers. To this friendship and to his acknowledged ability he undoubtedly owed his appointment in 1692. His associates on the commission were Nathaniel Saltonstall of Haverhill, Major Bartholomew Gedney, John Hathorne and Jonathan Corwin of Salem, Major John Richards, Wait Winthrop, Peter Sargent and Capt. Samuel Sewall, of Boston. Saltonstall withdrew soon after his appointment, probably immediately after the first sitting of the court, at which Bridget Bishop was tried, because he was " very much dissatisfied with the proceedings of it." [5]

The men who constituted this commission, or court, were among the ablest in the colony. None stood higher in the social scale ; none in the colony were better qualified for the work of the bench. On the great question of the hour, they entertained substantially the same views as the jurists of England, and in their subsequent acts were governed by the rules laid down by the English courts in numerous cases, although

4 Bancroft's Hist. U. S., II., 258.
5 Brattle, Mass. Hist. Coll., I-V., 75.

JUDGE SAMUEL SEWALL.

COTTON MATHER.

possibly they did not always protect the rights
of accused persons as carefully as the English
judges did.   Thomas Newton, a trained lawyer,
was appointed special king's attorney for the
trial of the witchcraft cases, and prepared the
earlier ones for the court, after which he resigned and the attorney general, Anthony
Checkley, took charge of the prosecution.
Checkley had been attorney general since 1689,
having been first chosen by "the governor,
council and assembly," in that year and recom-
missioned by Phips on July 27, 1692.   The
fact that none of these judges were educated for
the bar has been emphasized by some writers on
the witchcraft troubles of 1692.   That is true,
but these men probably knew as much about the
law of witchcraft as any lawyers in America at
that time; perhaps more than most of them.
The cases were tried in accordance with distin-
guished English precedents, and it is very much
to be doubted whether the result would have been
any different had lawyers occupied the bench.
The office of sheriff was substituted for that of
marshal, and George Corwin, a relative of Jonathan Corwin, appointed to the new office.   Marshal Herrick was appointed a deputy sheriff.   Persons accused of witchcraft were committed to the
jails in Salem, Boston, Ipswich and Cambridge.
Most of those first committed by the magistrates to await the action of the higher court

were sent to Boston, as up to this time all capital trials had taken place there. After the trials were begun in Salem, prisoners were committed to the jail in that town.[6]

The preliminary trials or examinations of the accused were held in Nathaniel Ingersoll's tavern and in the meeting house in Salem Village, now Danvers ; in the meeting-house in the town of Salem on the site of the present First Church, or in Thomas Beadle's house, or tavern, on Essex street. Nearly all the accused were finally tried in the court house that stood in what was then Town-house lane, now Washington street, about opposite the end of Lynde street, Salem. Some, perhaps, were tried in the Salem meeting house.

There is a tradition that trials or examinations of some kind were held in the Roger Williams house on the corner of Essex and North streets. No direct evidence of this exists. The court of Oyer and Terminer never sat there. The house was occupied at the time by Jonathan Corwin, and no doubt complaints were there made to him against suspected persons, and warrants for their arrest issued. Possibly grand jury deliberations were held in the house while trials were being held in the court house. In all

6 The Salem jail was located on Prison Lane, now St. Peter street, on the corner of the present Federal street, and some of the timbers of the old building are contained in the frame of Mr. A. C. Goodell's house near this corner, on Federal street.

JUDGE CORWIN OR ROGER WILLIAMS HOUSE. (AS IT WAS ABOUT 1850.)

probability it had some connection with the witchcraft prosecutions. The tradition has been handed down with too much directness to admit of serious doubt.

Where were the witchcraft victims hanged? No one knows as matter of absolute certainty. The tradition has always been that Gallows hill, between Salem and Peabody, was the scene of the executions. No other place has ever been seriously suggested. The records do not throw light upon this question, but the tradition is hardly open to doubt. The earliest writings in which I find mention of this hill as the place of execution bear date about one hundred years after the event. Two lives might well have spanned that period — certainly three did in innumerable instances; so that the story could hardly have been misunderstood or misstated in those transmissions. A letter written in Salem, Nov. 25, 1791, by Rev. Dr. Holyoke, furnishes the following information : " In the last month there died a man in this town, by the name of John Symonds, aged a hundred years lacking about six months, having been born in the famous '92. He has told me that his nurse had often told him, that while she was attending his mother at the time she lay in with him, she saw from the chamber windows, those unhappy people hanging on Gallows hill, who were executed for witches by the delusion of the times." A family of the name of Symonds lived, many years ago, on Bridge street, Salem, near the bridge leading to Beverly. From that spot Gallows hill was plainly visible. Symonds families also lived in North Salem then, and the hill could be easily seen from there. A writer in the Salem Register about 1880, stated that an elderly citizen had told him that he had traced the ancient path to the summit of the hill. It did not lead from Boston street, as now, but from the old pasture entrance at the head of Broad street. This same elderly citizen remembered the oak tree that stood on the hill and had been used as a gallows, and pointed out the place where it stood in his younger days.*

The new court of Oyer and Terminer sat for the first time in Salem in June, for the purpose of trying Bridget Bishop. There are no complete records of this court now extant. Our information of its proceedings is obtained mainly from the loose papers on file in the court house

---

* After long and careful investigation I am convinced that the condemned persons were hanged near the head of what is now Nichols street, on the hill, a little to the south-east, perhaps; and the bodies were buried near the head of Hanson street. Caleb Buffum, who lived at the foot of the hill and made coffins, is said by his descendants to have assisted in conveying the bodies to the North river, whence they were taken away in boats by relatives or friends.

There was a tavern on the spot now occupied by the Nichols house at the head of Proctor's court, and there, on execution day, tradition in the Buffum family says, the crowd would· gather to drink and make merry, many getting drunk.

SITE OF COURT HOUSE (1692), SALEM.

in Salem and the state house in Boston.   Quite
a number of valuable and interesting papers
have, from time to time, been deposited with the
Essex Institute in Salem and the historical so-
cieties of Boston.   The dates of the sessions of
the court are found in the History of Massachusetts written by Gov. Hutchinson.   Hutchinson
is supposed to have had access to the court
record, but the dates which he mentions are un-
questionably misleading.   For instance, when
he says that six persons, whom he names, were
tried and convicted on August 5,[7] we know that
this was not possible.   It would take more than
a day to hear the testimony we now have in the
cases.   How much more there was then it is not
possible to say ; doubtless considerable.[8]   Some
time must have been consumed in empanelling
juries and returning and recording verdicts.
Still more, we know that much time was wasted
by reason of the " fits " and " afflictions " of the
witnesses and the accusers.   During the trial of
one of these very cases that Hutchinson alleges
was tried on August 5, the report says : " It cost
the court a wonderful deal of trouble to hear
the testimonies of the sufferers, for when they

7 Hist. Mass., II., 55-58.

8 Clerk Stephen Sewall wrote in the case of Rebecca Nurse :
" In this Tryall are Twenty Papers, besides this judgment &
there were in this tryall as well as other Tryalls of ye same nature severall evidences vive voce which were not written and
so I can give no copies of them."

were going to give in their depositions they
would for a long while be taken with fits, etc."
Thomas Newton, the attorney general, wrote to
the clerk : " I fear we shall not this week try
all we have sent for, by reason the trials will be
tedious, and the afflicted persons cannot readily
give their testimony, being struck dumb and
senseless for a season." The probability is that
the dates mentioned by Hutchinson and others
as days of trial, were the days on which sentence
was pronounced. August 5 was Friday ; September 9 was Friday, and September 17 was
Saturday. These would very naturally be sentence
days, but certainly not days on which the court
would come in to begin the trial of a half dozen
important cases. Furthermore, the papers on
file show that Burroughs, who, Hutchinson says
was tried on August 5, was on trial on the 2d
and 3rd of that month.[8] His trial probably was
begun on the 2d and was finished on or before
the 5th. Most testimony before the grand inquest was written down when given, and at the
jury trials read to the court and sworn to by
the witness. Sometimes it was called testimony
and at others, deposition.

The trial of Bridget Bishop was held the first

8 When I speak of "trials," I include the examinations before the grand jury, for most of the time was occupied in taking
testimony there. Before the jury of trials, when this testimony
was read, the afflicted often created scenes of confusion, and
had fits, and otherwise interrupted the proceedings.

COTTON MATHER'S GRAVE, BOSTON.

week in June. Most of the depositions and
testimony against her are dated June 2. This
was probably the date on which they were
taken before the grand jury not that of the day
they were given before the jury of trials. She
was convicted, and hanged on June 10, Friday.
The court then adjourned to the 28th of June.

The newly elected General Court convened in
Boston in the mean time, June 8. The judges,
before they resumed business, in accordance
with a time-honored custom, united with the
Governor and council in requesting the opinion
of the ministers of the churches in and around
Boston on the momentous question then pend-
ing. The answer, written by Cotton Mather,
was a calm, judicious paper. After acknowledg-
ing the success which God had given to " the
sedulous and assiduous endeavors of the rulers
to defeat the abominable witchcrafts," they
prayed that " the discovery of those mysterious
and mischievious wickednesses might be per-
fected." They continue :

"We judge that, in the prosecution of these and all
such witchcrafts there is need of a very critical and ex-
quisite caution, lest by too much credulity for things
received only upon the devil's authority, there be a door
opened for a long train of miserable consequences, and
Satan get an advantage over us ; for we should, not be
ignorant of his devices.

As in complaints upon witchcraft there may be matters
of inquiry which do not amount unto matters of presumption, and there may be matters of presumption which yet

may not be matters of conviction, so it is necessary that all proceedings thereabout be managed with an exceeding tenderness toward those that may be complained of, especially if they have been persons formerly of an unblemished reputation.

When the first inquiry is made into the circumstances of such as may lie under the just suspicion of witchcrafts, we could wish that there may be ad   tted as little as possible of such noise, company and openness as may too hastily expose them that are examined, and that there may be nothing used as a test for the trial of the suspected, the lawfulness whereof may be doubted by the people of God, but that the directions given by such judicious writers as Perkins and Barnard, may be observed.

Presumptions whereupon persons may be committed, and much more, convictions whereupon persons may be condemned as guilty of witchcrafts, ought certainly to be more considerable than barely the accused persons being represented by a spectre unto the afflicted, inasmuch as it is an undoubted and notorious thing, that a demon may by God's permission appear, even to ill purposes, in the shape of an innocent, yea, and a virtuous man. Nor can we esteem alterations made in the sufferers, by a look or touch of the accused, to be an infallible: evidence of guilt, but frequently liable to be abused by the devil's legerdemain.

We know not whether some remarkable affronts given the devils, by our disbelieving these testimonies whose whole force and strength is from them alone, may not put a period unto the progress of the dreadful calamity begun upon us, in the accusation of so many persons, whereof some, we hope, are yet clear from the great transgression laid to their charge.

Nevertheless, we cannot but humbly recommend unto the government, the speedy and vigorous prosecutions of such as have rendered themselves obnoxious, according to the directions given in the laws of God and the wholesome statutes of the English nation for the detection of witchcrafts.''

Many writers, in commenting on this letter of

advice, lay particular stress on the last clause, often ignoring the others. Many have quoted that alone as indicating the views of the ministers. Could anything be more unjust? The whole history of the witchcraft era, and especially the part the ministers took in it, has been warped by such perversion of this letter. Read without prejudice, is it not more like the charge of a judge to a jury than a savage demand for the shedding of innocent blood, as many historians would have us believe? Five of the six paragraphs in the letter devoted to advice are cautionary, while only one urges that those who have violated the laws of God and man, as understood by every one then, be vigorously prosecuted. Unfortunately, the judges did not heed the cautions. They were more blinded than the ministers. As Barrett Wendell says, it was " an honest warning of a danger in spite of which the court had no moral right to hesitate in the performance of its official duty."[9]

The court reconvened the last of June, and tried Sarah Good, Sarah Wildes, Elizabeth Howe and Susanna Martin, and finished the trial of Rebecca Nurse, begun on June 2d and continued on the 3rd. All were convicted, and sentenced to be hanged on Tuesday, July 19. The third sitting was about August 2, Tuesday, when Rev. George Burroughs, John Procter, Elizabeth

9 " Cotton Mather," 108.

Procter, George Jacobs, sen., John Willard and Martha Carrier were tried and convicted. With the exception of Elizabeth Procter, they were executed on Friday, August 19. Another session was held early in September, beginning on Tuesday, the 6th, and terminating on Saturday, the 17th. Martha Corey, Mary Easty, Alice Parker, Ann Pudeator, Dorcas Hoar and Mary Bradbury were tried, found guilty and sentenced the first week. All save the two last named were hanged on the 22d.

During the following week nine more accused persons were convicted and sentenced, namely : Margaret Scott, Wilmot Reed, Samuel Wardwell, Mary Parker, Abigail Faulkner, Rebecca Eames, Mary Lacey, Ann Foster and Abigail Hobbs. Scott, Reed, Wardwell and Parker were executed on Thursday, the 22d. These, with the four convicted the preceding week, were the last persons hanged for witchcraft in 1692 or, for that matter, ever in Massachusetts. It was on this occasion that Rev. Mr. Noyes, minister of the First Church in Salem, turned toward the bodies of the victims and said : " What a sad thing it is to see eight firebrands of hell hanging there." [10]   Hutchinson says, " Those who were condemned and were not executed, I suppose all confessed their guilt. I have seen the confessions of several of them."[11]

10 Calef. Fowler's Ed., 265.   11 Hist. Mass., II., 59.

After these convictions, the court adjourned the witchcraft trials until Nov. 2. But it never sat again to try witchcraft cases. It did sit in Boston on Oct. 10, to " trie a French malatto for shooting dead an English youth." [12] On the 28th of the preceding June the General Court passed an act establishing courts of general sessions of the peace on and after the last Tuesday in July, which was the 26th ; also establishing inferior courts of common pleas to hold sessions at the same time and in places where they were formerly held. This act was disallowed by the home government on Aug. 22, 1695. These courts were established only until others should be provided. At the session of the General Court in the fall an act was passed, on Nov. 25, creating various courts, among them courts of quarter sessions and common pleas and a superior court of judicature. On the 16th of December, a further act was passed which provided that, "considering the many persons in Essex county charged as capital offenders, and that the time had passed for the sitting of the court," a special court of assize and jail delivery was ordered in the county.[13] The first term of this court was to be held in Salem in January. These acts establishing regular courts certainly terminated the special court of Oyer and Terminer. Tribunals created in emergencies always ceased

12 Sewall Papers, I., 366.   13 Province Laws, I., 100.

to exist when the emergency was passed.[14] It
was now passed, because regular courts had been
established competent to do the work previously
done by the Commissioners of Oyer and Terminer. Stoughton was made chief justice of
the new court, with Richards, Winthrop, Sewall
and Danforth, associates. At its session held in
Salem in January, the grand jury found about
fifty indictments for witchcraft, and twenty-one
persons were tried. Three of them were convicted and sentenced to be hanged, viz., Mary
Post of Rowley, Elizabeth Johnson, junior, and
Sarah Wardwell, widow of Samuel Wardwell,
of Andover. They were never executed. Four
were tried in Charlestown, one in Boston, and
five in Ipswich in May (the last trials), but no
more convictions could be secured. Finally, in
May, Gov. Phips issued a proclamation releasing
all persons held in custody on charge of witchcraft— about one hundred and fifty in number.[15]
No other prosecutions for witchcraft were ever
made in Essex county.

Only one case of witchcraft ever after occurred in Massachusetts. That was in 1693.
Cotton Mather says : " It was upon the Lord's
day, the 10th of September, in the year 1693,
that Margaret Rule, after some hours of previous
disturbance in the public assembly, fell into odd

14 Hale, P. C., II., 4.
15 Phips to Nottingham, Essex Inst. Hist. Coll. IX., pt. 2, 81.

fits, which caused her friends to carry her home,
where her fits grew in a few hours into a figure
that satisfied the spectators of their being pre-
ternatural." He says further that the young
woman was assaulted by eight cruel spectres.
" These spectres brought unto her a book and
demanded of her that she would set her hand to
it or touch it at least with her hand, as a sign of
her becoming a servant of the devil.   Upon her
refusal to do what they asked they did not re-
new the proffers of the book unto her, but fell
to tormenting her 'in a manner too hellish
to be sufficiently described'." The " afflictions "
of Margaret Rule continued six weeks. " At
last," says Mather, " being as it were tired with
their ineffectual attempts to mortify her they
furiously said, ' Well, you shan't be the last.'
And after a pause they added, ' Go, and the
devil go with you, we can do no more,' whereupon they flew out of the room, and she, returning perfectly to herself, most affectionately gave
thanks to God for her deliverance." Calef says
that in answer to a question one of Margaret's
friends said : " She does not eat at all, but
drinks rum." Fowler says she " had a bad
case of delirium tremens."[16]

Dwight, in his " Travels," tells of a case al-

16 See Mather's account of the " Sufferings of Margaret
Rule," and Calef's comments, quoted by Fowler in his " Salem
Witchcraft, etc.," pp. 25-27.

leged to have happened in Northampton after 1692, where one man accused another of witchcraft, and the case came before Magistrate Partridge. The magistrate said this case came under the head of offences where the accuser "received half of what was adjudged. A person accused of witchcraft was by law punished with twenty stripes. He should therefore order ten of those to the accuser." The trouble with this story is that the punishment for witchcraft was not "twenty stripes." It is far more likely that the magistrate ordered the stripes because he believed the accuser had made a false accusation.

A Benom woman and her daughter, aged thirteen, of Hartford, Conn., were tried on charge of witchcraft in 1697 and acquitted. Ten cases of the crime or disorder occurred in Connecticut in all.

It is quite possible that other cases occurred in different parts of the country, but the early records are too imperfect to be implicitly relied upon.

Nineteen persons had been hanged in Salem during the four months; Giles Corey had been pressed to death for refusing to plead; and Sarah Osburn and Ann Foster had died in prison from ill-treatment and exposure. Add to these the number of those who had been released because they confessed, those who had escaped, or been bailed, or otherwise gone free, and the total number accused and arrested must have been more than two hundred and fifty.

What led the Governor to issue this proclamation? What caused him "to put an end to the witchcraft prosecutions?" It has been often asserted in substance, that "the eyes of the Governor" and "the eyes of the people" were opened to the error of their way when Mrs. Hale, wife of the minister at Beverly, was accused. One writer says this was what finally broke the spell.[18] Let us see. Mrs. Hale's name was mentioned, or "whispered about," in October, 1692. Yet when, a few weeks later, the court was reconstructed,—for that was all it amounted to,—it was composed of men, all but one of whom had been members of the court of Oyer and Terminer. All save Danforth were known to be in full sympathy with witchcraft prosecutions. That there might be no question about the right of this tribunal to hang witches, the general court in October, re-enacted the colonial statute against witchcraft, and in December re-enforced it with the English statute.[19] The new court resumed the business in Salem, as already stated, in the most vigorous manner, with a zeal not exceeded by the tribu-

18 Salem Witchcraft, II., 345.
19 Notes on Hist. Witchcraft in Mass., Moore, 9.

nal which preceded it. Every effort was made
by the authorities for three months longer to
secure convictions. Does this look as if the
spell had been broken in October? Does this
look as if the prosecutions had been brought
to a close because Mrs. Hale had been "named,"
and other persons of high connections "suspected?" The officials, who would, under those
circumstances, have been the first to abate in
zeal, never relaxed their efforts until the juries,
composed of the common people, had refused
repeatedly to convict. The juries that tried the
accused in 1692 were composed of freemen only,
while those of 1693 were chosen from among all
those inhabitants who possessed the requisite
amount of property to qualify them as electors
under the new charter.[20] Freemen were necessarily church members and not as likely to act
independently as the jurors selected from substantially the whole body of the people. It is
evident that during the period between September 17, when the court of Oyer and Terminer
sat for the last time, and the opening of the
session of the Superior Court the following January, the people generally began to emerge from
the long night-mare, the panic, into which they
had been thrown. The inhabitants of Andover
were among the first to protest, uniting in a re-

[20] Further notes on the Hist. of Witchcraft, etc., Goodell,
1884, p. 33; Also, Province Laws, 1692-93, chap. 33.

monstrance to the General Court against the witchcraft proceedings, and even bringing suits against some of their accusers. Spectral evi· dence lost its force, and finally was entirely rejected, leaving nothing to substantiate the charges. All other convictions had been secured largely on this species of evidence.* One thing is impressed on our minds as we study the history of these trials : and that is, that such proceedings would not be allowed in any court in this country in our day. Granting that all that is said in criticism of the "red tape" requirements of our modern courts is true, yet, as Hon. W. D. Northend has said : " under the rules of law as now fully established none of the evidence upon which convictions were found would be admitted. Spectral and kindred evidence could not be allowed, and without it not one of the accused could have been convicted.[21]

There is evidence that Gov. Phips was never in full sympathy with the modes of procedure in the witchcraft prosecutions. Being unlearned in law and theology, he seems to have followed

* When the chief judge gave the first jury their charge, he told them that they were not to mind whether the bodies of the said afflicted were really pined and consumed as was expressed in the indictment; but whether the said afflicted did not suffer from the accused such affliction as naturally tended to their being pined and consumed, wasted, &c. This, said he, is a pining and consuming in the sense of the law." Brattle's Letter, Mass. Hist. Coll. 1st series, V., 77.

21 Essex Inst., Hist. Coll., XX., 270.

the advice of the judges and the more bigoted of the ministers. In his letter to the home government, under date of October 14, 1692, the Governor says he was prevailed upon by the clamors of the friends of the afflicted and the advice of the deputy governor (Stoughton) to give a commission of Oyer and Terminer; that he was absent in the eastern part of the country almost the whole time, and depended upon the judgment of the court as to a method of proceeding in cases of witchcraft.[22] He returned from the east about October 12. It seems always to have been a question whether the governor "decided to abolish the court" for the purpose of putting an end to the witchcraft prosecutions. It is evident that he was dissatisfied with its method of procedure. He may have thought the work could be done by the regular courts. But if he dissolved it to put an end to those prosecutions, would he have reappointed the same men to the new court and allowed them to continue the trials with unabated zeal? If Phips really abolished this court, if it did not fall solely because of the constituting of a new tribunal with jurisdiction over the same class of cases with which it had dealt, then is it not more probable that he dissolved it because the people were complaining bitterly of the arbitrary manner in which it had

22 Phips to Nottingham, Essex Inst. Hist. Coll., IX., pt. 2, 81.

been constituted, and the arbitrary manner in which it had proceeded with its work ? This view is strengthened by Phips' letter to the home government, in which he says that when he came home from the war in the east he found many persons in a strange ferment of dissatisfaction.[23] The Governor himself says he issued his freedom proclamation because he had been informed by the King's attorney general that " some of ye cleared and ye condemned were under ye same circumstances or that there was ye same reason to clear ye three condemned as ye rest according to his judgement."[24] He further states that the judges, when he appointed them to the new court, promised to proceed after another method, by which he meant that convictions were not to be secured on spectral evidence.[25] He does not at any time question the validity of the Commission of Oyer and Terminer nor of the Superior Court, nor the reality of witchcraft. All complaints are directed against modes of precedure. That the accusations made against so many people of high character and irreproachable life led to grave doubts whether the devil did not take the shapes of persons without their knowledge or consent, to afflict his victims, there can be no question. But there is no evidence that at this time any one doubted that there was such a thing as

23 Ibd.   24 Phips to Nottingham, Feb. 21, 1693.   25 Ibd.

witchcraft. Even Calef, the great critic of
Mather and the judges, wrote as late as November, 1693 : "That there are witches is not the
doubt. The scriptures else were vain which as-
signs their punishment to be by death, but what
this witchcraft is and wherein it does consist,
seems to be the whole difficulty." [26]

On Oct. 11, 1692, Henry Selpins and Peter
Pietrus, ministers of New York, Godfrey Delius,
minister of the Dutch church at New Albany,
Rudolph Varich, minister at Flatbush, answered
certain questions propounded to them by Gov.
Dudley of New York on behalf of the Massachusetts authorities, "for guidance in future
trials there." They said, that there was such a
thing as witchcraft; that "the formal essence
of witchcraft consists in an alliance with the
Devil"; that "the spectre or apparition of one
who immediately works violence and injury upon the afflicted is by no means sufficient to convict a witch or wizzard, although preceded by
enmity or threats. The reason is because the
Devil can assume the shape of a good man. An
honest and charitable life and conduct, probably
removes the suspicion of criminal intent from
those who are accused of witchcraft by the testimony of the afflicted. Still, this is not an
indubitable evidence of false accusation because a cunning man might conceal his devilish

26 Fowler's ed., 62.

practices under the semblance of a good life in order to escape suspicion, and righteous condemnation. It is possible for those who are really tortured, convulsed and afflicted by the Devil with many miseries, during several months, to suffer no wasting of body and no weakening of their spirits. The reason is that nutrition is perfect, the stomach suffers no injury."

This information may have been asked for by the Lieutenant Governor, or by the Governor himself during one of his brief visits to Boston that summer. Whether the letter influenced the Governor in his subsequent action, it is not possible to say with certainty. Quite likely it did to some extent. On the whole, notwithstanding the letters of Gov. Phips to the home government, it is not entirely clear just what motives prompted his acts during the fall and winter of 1692-3. In some respects they were inconsistent with one another, and far from being in accord with his written statements.

THE GILES COREY MILL, DANVERS.

GALLOWS HILL, SALEM.

CHAPTER V.

MARTHA AND GILES COREY.

WELVE days after Good, Osburn and Tituba were sent to jail, warrants were issued for Martha Corey, wife of Giles Corey. She was immediately taken into custody, and on March 21 examined before Hathorne and Corwin. Martha Corey was, upon all the evidence that has come down to us, a woman of more than average judgment and discretion. From the beginning, she resolutely and persistently denounced the whole witchcraft business. While her husband was, at first, completely carried away with the storm which swept over the rural community, she had no faith in it. She sought to persuade him not to attend the hearings, nor to countenance the prosecutions in any manner. It was charged against her that she took the saddle off his horse on one occasion when he was preparing to go to the examinations. Giles Corey was eighty years of age, and although Martha was his third wife and no doubt somewhat his junior, she was probably more than sixty years

of age at this time. She joined the Village
church in 1690,[1] he the Salem church in 1691. It
has always seemed a little singular that a
woman of her character should be among the
first to be accused. Whether her early and earnest protest led to the use of her name among
the suspected, has always been a question. It
may have aroused a suspicion that she was in
league with the evil one.

When the name of Martha Corey was first
whispered around by the girls of the accusing
circle, Edward Putnam and Ezekiel Cheever
paid a visit to her. They sought to secure from
this old woman some sort of confession. It was
on March 12. On the way, they called at Ann
Putnam's, to see what assistance she could ren-
der. Asked about the clothes Corey wore when
she appeared on her spectral visits, Ann replied that she had just made one of those calls,
but had so blinded her that she could not see
what clothes she wore. These " detectives "
then rode on to Corey's. On their arrival, Martha said to them: " I know what you have come
for. You are come to talk with me about being
a witch, but I am none. I cannot help people's
talking about me." She inquired whether the
afflicted had attempted to describe her clothes.
That she should so accurately divine the object

1 See Church Record; also, Mass. Hist. Coll., 3rd series, III.,
169.

of their call was by them, and the court subsequently, deemed conclusive evidence of her being a witch. Undoubtedly she had heard that her name was being "taken" by the afflicted. So, too, she may have known that the children commonly told what sort of clothes the spectral visitors wore when making their visits. The conversation was protracted, Putnam and Cheever from their own account, endeavoring by every means in their power to get some statement from Martha Corey which could be used against her. Regarding what they said to her they testified : " She made but little answer to this but seemed to smile at it as if she had showed us a pretty trick. She told us that she did not think that there were any witches. Wee told her wee were fully satisfied about the first three that they were such persons they were accused for, shee said if they were wee could not blame the devill for making witches of them, for they were idle sloathfull persons and minded nothing that was good." On the way home, Putnam and Cheever made another call on Ann. She told them that Goodwife Corey had not appeared to her during their absence.[2] Did she shrewdly volunteer this statement, that they might not again ask her about the clothes Corey wore at any particular time? It is, however, pretty dangerous to attempt to read the minds

2 Essex Court Records.

of those who lived centuries before us by the
knowledge we have of their acts, and that
knowledge but partial and imperfect. And yet,
the tenor of Ann Putnam's acts all through
these trials was such as to justify very strong
suspicions as to her honesty. The examination
of Martha Corey was a sample of cross-examin-
ation and brow-beating on the part of the magistrates, which finds parallel only in the conduct
of some ungentlemanly shyster lawyer of a type
happily now very rare. It was quite extended,
but confined mainly to an effort to make the
prisoner confess. She persisted in denying.
Here are some samples :

Mr. Hathorne. You are now in the hands of authority.
Tell me, now, why you hurt these persons.—I do not.
Hathorne. Who doth ?—Pray give me leave to go to
prayer. This request was made sundry times.
Hathorne. We do not send for you to go to prayer, but
tell me why you hurt these.—I am an innocent person. I
never had to do with witchcraft since I was born. I am a
gospel woman. * * * *
Hathorne. How could you tell, then, that the child was
bid to observe what clothes you wore when some one came
to speak with you? Cheever interrupted her and bid her
not begin with a lie, and so Edward Putnam declared the
matter.
Hathorne. Who told you that ?—He said the child said.
Cheever. You speak falsely.—Then Edward Putnam
read again.
Hathorne. Why did you ask if the child asked what
clothes you wore ?—My husband told me the others told.
Hathorne. Goodman Corey, did you tell her? The old
man denied that he told her so.

Hathorne. Did you not say your husband told you so?
No answer. * * * *
Hathorne. You dare thus to lie in all this assembly.
You are now before authority. I expect the truth. You
promised it. Speak now and tell who told you what
clothes.—Nobody.

At one time the children cried out that a man
was whispering in her ear. Hathorne asked:
"What did he say to you?" She replied: "We
must not believe all that these distracted children say." When she denied any charge made
against her there was "extreme agony of all the
afflicted."

Parris, who reported this trial, says, "It was
noted when she bit her lip several of the afflicted were bitten." Also, "when her hands
were at liberty the afflicted were pinched."
Hathorne asked: "Do you not see these children
and women are rational and sober when your
hands are fastened?" "Immediately they were
seized with fits, and the standers-by said she was
squeezing her fingers, her hands being eased by
them that held them on purpose for trial.
Quickly after, the marshall said, 'She hath bit
her lip,' and immediately the afflicted were in an
uproar." Throughout her examination she was
badgered by Hathorne, badgered by Corwin,
badgered by Rev. Mr. Noyes, badgered by the
marshal and by the audience.

The following document is on file in the
court house in Salem :

Giles Choree testifieth and saith that in the evening, sitting by the fire, my wife asked me to go to bed. I told (her) I would go to prayer & when I went to prayer I could nott utter my desires with any sense, not open my mouth to speak. My wife did percieve itt & came towards me & said she was coming to me. After this in a little space I did according to my measure attend the duty. Some time last week I fetched an ox well out of the woods about noon & he laying down in the yard I went to raise him to yoke him but he could not rise but draged his hinder parts as if he had been hip shott but after did rise. I had a catt some times last week strangely taken on the suddam, & did make me think she would have died presently, my wife bid me knock her in the head butt I did not and since she is well. Another time going to duties I was interrupted for a space butt afterwards I was helpt according to my poor measure. My wife hath been wont to sitt up after I went to bed & I have percieved her to kneel down on the hearth as if she were at prayer but heard nothing. *At the examination of Sarah Good* & others my wife was willing

Here the statement ceases. Some writers attempt to discredit it as not given in the usual and regular way. Because a line is drawn through the words italicised above, they think some suspicion attaches to it, and that the parties who tried to get the old man to testify against his wife discovered that they could not draw anything derogatory from him, and there was danger that his evidence would be favorable to her. Is it not more probable that the recorder was interrupted at this point and did not then complete the statement; that afterwards he started to erase the uncompleted line, or, perhaps, meant the mark he made to be an erasure?

There appears to be no evidence in connection with this paper to prove that it was not testimony taken in court in the usual way. Its date is four days after the examination of Martha Corey, it is true ; but may it not have been given in then? Evidence would not be admitted in such an irregular manner to-day, but the practices of the courts were much different in 1692. During the examination, Mrs. Pope threw her muff at the prisoner, but did not hit her. Then she pulled off her shoe and, throwing it, struck Mrs. Corey in the head. This Mrs. Pope was an important witness in many cases, but subsequently acknowledged her error and deplored the whole business. Martha Corey was committed for trial. She was tried by the court at its September sitting, convicted, and sentenced on September 10, and executed on September 22. Calef says, " Martha Corey, wife of Giles Corey, protesting her innocency, concluded her life with an eminent prayer upon the ladder."[3]

After her sentence, and while awaiting execution, Parris, accompanied by Lieut. Nathaniel Putnam and two deacons of his church, visited her in jail and pronounced the sentence of excommunication upon her.[4]

[3] Fowler's ed., 262.
[4] " Accordingly, this 14 September, 1692, the three aforesaid brethren went with the pastor to her in Salem Prison ; whom we found very obdurate, justifying herself, and condemning all

The case of Giles Corey is, in some respects, the most interesting and the most tragic in all this wonderful drama of witchcraft. As previously stated, he was carried away with the delusion from the outset, and against the wishes of his wife, attended the earlier examinations. He was arrested on a warrant issued April 18, and examined on the 19th, in the Village meeting house. The accusing girls conducted themselves in the usual manner, and were so badly affected "with fits and troubled with pinches" that the court ordered Corey's hands to be tied. When the magistrates asked him if it was not enough to "act witchcraft at other times, but must you do it now in face of authority?" he replied, "I am poor creature and cannot help it." Later, the magistrate exclaimed: "Why do you tell such wicked lies against witnesses?" "One of his hands was let go," continues the record, "and several were afflicted. He held his head on one side, and then the heads of several of the afflicted were held on one side. He drew in his cheeks, and the cheeks of some of the afflicted were sucked in."

Elizabeth Woodwell deposed that she saw him

that had done anything to her just discovery or condemnation. Whereupon, after a little discourse (for her imperiousness would not suffer much), and after prayer, which she was willing to decline—the dreadful sentence of excommunication was pronounced against her." Extract from Parris' record in the church book, Mass. Hist. Coll., 3d series, III., 169.

on a lecture day come in and sit in the middle-most seat of the men's seats by the post. Mary Warren said he was hostile to her and afflicted her because he thought she caused John Procter to ask more for a piece of meadow than he was willing to give. John Derick, sixteen years of age, testified that "said Giles Corey came about the 20th of August and told me that he wanted some platers for he was gowen to have a feast he told me that he had a good mind to ask my dame but he said that she would not let him have them so he took the platers and cared them away being gown about half a oure with them then he brot them againe gowen away and said nothing." If Corey was going as a spectre why did he wish the actual platters? It is another case of bodily, material presence like that of Abigail Hobbs.

This testimony was given on September 7 before the grand inquest. There is very little evidence in Giles Corey's case. That given here comprises all of special interest. The magistrates committed him to jail. This was on or about April 18. He was brought before the court in September, to plead to an indictment for witchcraft. The old man refused to plead, "stood mute," as the law terms it. The records of the Salem church under date of September 18, Sunday, state that, " G. Corey was excommunicated. The cause of it was, that he being accused and indicted for the sin of witchcraft, he refused to plead, and so incurred the sentence and penalty of *pain fortdure*, being undoubtedly guilty of the sin of witchcraft, or of throwing himself upon sudden and certain death, if he were otherwise innocent." Th does not say the penalty was enforced, only that it was incurred.

The English law of those days, for " standing mute " was that the prisoner " be remanded to the prison from whence he came and put into a low dark chamber, and there be laid on his back on the bare floor, naked, unless where decency forbids ; that there be placed upon his body as great a weight of iron as he could bear, and more, that he have no sustenance, save only on the first day, three morsels of the worst bread, and on the second day, three draughts of standing water, that should be nearest to the prison door, and in this situation this should be alternately his daily diet till he died, or—as anciently the judgement ran—till he answered."[5]

No other instance of the enforcement of this penalty is known in New England history. Blackstone says it was adopted in England about the beginning of the rein of Henry IV. He adds that the uncertainty of its origin, the doubts of its legality, and the repugnance of its theory to the humanity of the laws of England

5 Chitty's Blackstone, IV., 265.

all concurred to require the abolishment of the cruel punishment, so that standing mute should amount only to a confession of guilt.[6]

There is some uncertainty as to the place where the last act in this terrible tragedy took place. The tradition has always been that it was between the Howard street burial ground and Brown street, in an open field, and that Corey urged the officers to add more weight, that his misery might the sooner be ended, a request perfectly natural for a man who had made up his mind to die that way. Calef is authority for this story of monstrous brutality on the part of the officers : " In pressing, his tongue being pressed out of his mouth, the sheriff with his cane forced it in again when he was dying."[7] Sewall left this record : " Monday, September 19, 1692. About noon at Salem, Giles Corey was pressed to death for standing Mute ; much pains was used with him two days, one after another, by the court and Capt. Gardner of Nantucket who had been of his acquaintance, but all in vain."[8] This horrible tragedy was enacted three days previous to the hanging of Martha Corey and her nine companions. No one knows just why Corey refused to plead and suffered such a death. It may have been because of his stubborn nature and firm will, but more probably it was to save the attaint of his family and

6 Ibd., 266.   7 Fowler's ed., 260.   8 Sewall Papers, I., 364.

the forfeiture of his property, which would follow conviction if he pleaded. From what he
had seen of previous trials, he probably concluded that conviction was certain in his case,
especially if he had made up his mind not to
confess. While lying in jail he drew up and
executed a paper which he intended should op-
erate as a will, but which was in reality a deed

ANN PUTNAM HOUSE, DANVERS.

of conveyance. By it he conveyed all his property to William Cleeves and John Moulton, his
sons-in-law. The day after Corey's death
Thomas Putnam sent to Judge Sewall the following communication :

Last night my daughter Ann was grieviously tormented by witches, threatening that she should be pressed to death before Giles Corey ; but through the goodness of a gracious God, she had, at last, a little respite. Whereupon there appeared unto her (she said) a man in a winding sheet who told her that Giles Corey had murdered him by pressing him to death with his feet ; but that the devil then appeared unto him and covenanted with him and promised him that he should not be hanged. The apparition said God hardened his heart that he should not hearken to the advice of the court, and so die an easy death; because, as it said, it must be done to him as he had done to me. The apparition also said that Giles Corey was carried to the court for this and that the jury had found the murder ; and that her father knew the man and the thing was done before she was born.

This letter needs a little explanation. Corey appears to have been a man who, in early life if not in later, did about as he pleased in the com. munity, and had little consideration for the rights of others or for their feelings. He became involved in law suits, and even got into the criminal courts.[9] Jacob Goodell who worked for him was carried home sick by Martha Corey, and soon after died. The gossips said his death was caused by a beating which Corey gave him. The coroner's jury said the man had been bruised to death, " having clodders of blood about the heart." This was about 1676. To this case Thomas Putnam refers in the above quoted statement. The affair did happen before

9 " Giles Coree being presented upon suspicion of abusing the body of Jacob Goodell is fined." Essex County Court Records, Salem, 1676.

Ann Putnam was born, but the arrest of Corey
and his subsequent horrible death must have
revived all the old stories about him.   No doubt
Ann heard them at this time, and they were
sure, under the circumstances, to lose nothing in
the re-telling.   Corey was also before the court
in 1678 on suspicion of having set fire to John
Procter's house.   His innocence was clearly
proved, and he turned on Procter and other of
his defamers and sued them, recovering from all
of them.   He had had a lawsuit with Procter
previous to this.[10]   In other ways he was mixed
up unpleasantly in neighborhood affairs.
Whether these controversies had anything to do
with his prosecution for witchcraft in 1692, or
the severity with which he was dealt, I am unable to say.   Their revival would not aid him,
certainly.   Sewall says of the charge that Corey
stamped and pressed a man to death, that
" 'twas not remembered till Ane Putnam was
told of it by said Corey's spectre the Sabbath
night before the execution."[11]   It is hardly possible that a man could be arrested and dealt
with in the manner Corey was and no one remember and recall that fourteen and sixteen
years before he had been charged with murder
and arson.

10 " John Prokter against Giles Corye, defendant in an action
of appeal from a judgement of Maj. Hathorne in August last,
the jury found for the defendant, the confirmation of the former judgement."   Essex County Court Records, Salem.

11 Sewall Papers, I., 364.

CHAPTER VI.

THE STORY OF REBECCA NURSE.

REBECCA Nurse was born in Yarmouth, England, and baptised there on February 21, 1621. This would make her 71 years of age at the time of the witchcraft troubles. She was daughter of William Towne and wife of Francis Nurse of Salem Village. Nurse lived from about 1638 to 1678 near what is now Skerry street in the city of Salem. His occupation was that of tray-maker. In 1678 he purchased the farm in Salem Village then known as the Townsend Bishop farm, now better known as the Nurse farm.

The history of the place is this: Townsend Bishop, on January 16, 1636, received a grant of 300 acres of land in the Village. On this he built a substantial house. That house is standing to-day, and is the widely known Rebecca Nurse house. Its identity is proved beyond question by documentary evidence. Bishop sold the estate in 1641, to Henry Chickering, who in turn sold it to Governor Endicott in 1648 for

REBECCA NURSE HOUSE, DANVERS.

£160. Endicott gave the farm to his son John
in 1653, but did not execute the deed until 1662.
The governor died in 1665, and a lawsuit followed over the will. It was finally settled by
the general court in favor of young John and
his wife. John died in 1668, and his widow
married in August of that year, Rev. James
Allen, a minister of the First Church in Boston.
She died in 1673, and thus the Bishop farm became the property of Allen, who sold it to
Nurse in 1678 for £400. Nurse was to have
twenty-one years in which to pay for the property, paying in the meantime an annual rental
of £7 a year during the first twelve years and
£10 for each remaining year.

The Nurses were blessed with eight children,
Samuel, John, Francis and Benjamin, Rebecca,
wife of Thomas Preston, Mary, wife of John Tarbell, Elizabeth, wife of William Russell, and
Sarah, then unmarried. They dwelt on the farm
or near it, and in a short time Nurse divided the
larger part among them.[1] From all the information that has come down to us, Salem Village
contained no more prosperous, happy and con-
tented family than this. There were others of
much greater wealth, but none that promised
more enjoyment in old age than that reared and

[1] For the information about the Bishop-Nurse farm, also
for an account of the lawsuit which followed the purchase, I
am indebted to the diligent researches of Mr. Upham.

established at Salem Village by Francis Nurse and his wife Rebecca. He had been prominent and honored in the communities where he dwelt. She was an intelligent, pious, devout woman, a veritable " mother in Israel." Against her good name and fair fame no breath of suspicion had yet been uttered. The first trouble appears to have come to this family soon after the purchase of the Bishop farm. Allen had guaranteed the title. He was soon called upon to defend it against the claims of Zerubabel Endicott, who claimed a boundary line to the Endicott possessions that pushed back the eastern bounds of the Bishop farm. The controversy was a long one, going finally to the General Court for settlement. It was decided against Endicott. Nurse, to be sure, was only indirectly interested in the suit. Allen was the principal, and he kept his promise to defend the title. Nathaniel Putnam became involved in the suit. Some writers allege that Nurse thus incurred his hostility and that this was one of the incentives to the subsequent prosecution of Rebecca Nurse. It would seem that Putnam, if anything, was united with Allen and Nurse in fighting Endicott. It is even less likely that the Topsfield controversy engendered ill-feeling between the Village people and the Nurse family which lasted until witchcraft days. This affair may as well be narrated at this point.

In 1636 the General Court defined the bounds of Salem, Ipswich and Newbury as extending six miles into the country, measuring from their respective meeting houses. Three years later, the same power, in consideration that the inhabitants of Salem had agreed to plant a village near the river that runs to Ipswich, ordered that all lands near their bounds between Salem and the river, not belonging to any person or town by former grant, should belong to said village. The farmers of Salem Village thereupon began to push settlements beyond the six-mile limit. They cleared the forests and built houses. In 1643 the General Court, unmindful of its grant to the Salem Village people, authorized the inhabitants of Ipswich to locate on the same territory and establish a village. The town of Ipswich was incorporated October 18, 1650, and in 1658 a portion of the disputed land was made a part of the town. This brought into direct conflict the Village men, who had taken up lands under the vote of the General Court in 1639, and those who settled under the act of 1643. John Putnam of the Village and others of his great family and of the settlement met the Easteys and Townes of Topsfield on the disputed ground and had angry words with them. Not until 1728, when the town of Middleton was incorporated, to include most of the disputed territory from the Village and Topsfield, was the dispute settled.

Isaac Easty's wife was sister of Rebecca Nurse. The Townes, John and Joseph, jr., were nearly related to her. While most of the inhabitants of the Village took sides against the Topsfield men, the Nurse family supported them. When the Village meeting passed a protest against the Topsfield claim, Samuel Nurse, Rebecca's oldest son, and Thomas Preston, her son-in-law, entered their written dissent. Whether this long and bitter controversey had anything to do with the prosecution of Rebecca Nurse and Mary Easty is left to conjecture. It is certain that Thomas Preston joined with Thomas and Edward Putnam in signing the complaint against Sarah Good in 1692. Does not this indicate that whatever ill-feelings arose from the Topsfield feud, thirty years before, had been entirely forgotten, or at least forgiven?

The complaint against Rebecca Nurse was made by these same Putnams, Thomas and Edward. They complained against her for "vehement suspicion of having committed sundry acts of witchcraft" upon Mrs. Ann Putnam, Ann Putnam, jr., and Abigail Williams. The justices issued their warrant on March 23. On the following day Marshal Herrick made return that he had "apprehended the within named Rebecca Nurse and lodged her at Nathaniel Ingersoll's." The examination took place on the 24th. The record of that examination, as made by Rev.

Samuel Parris at the request of the magistrates, was as follows :

What do you say (speaking to one of the afflicted), have you seen this woman hurt you?—Yes, she beat me this morning.

Abigail, have you been hurt by this woman? Yes.

Ann Putnam in a grievous fit cried out, that she hurt her.

Goody Nurse, here are two, Ann Putnam the child and Abigail Williams, complain of your hurting them. What do you say to it?—I can say before my eternal father I am innocent and God will clear my innocency. Here is never a one in the assembly but desires it. But if you be guilty, pray God discover you.

Then Hen. Kenny rose up to speak. Goodm. Kenny, what do you say? Then he entered his complaint and farther said that since this Nurse came into the house he was seized twice with an amas'd condition. Here are not only these but here is ye wife of Mr. Thomas Putnam who accuseth you by credible information & that both of tempting her to iniquity and of greatly hurting her.—I am innocent & clear & have not been able to get out of doors these 8 or 9 days.

Mr. Putnam, give in what you have to say. Then Mr. Edward Putnam gave in his relate.

Is this true, Goody Nurse?—I never afflicted no child, never in my life.

You see these accuse you. Is it true?—No.

Are you an innocent person relating to this witchcraft? Here Thomas Putnam's wife cried out, did you not bring the black man with you? Did you not bid me tempt God and dye? How oft have you eat and drunk your own damnation.

What do you say to them?—O Lord, help me—and spread out her hands & the afflicted were grieviously vexed.

* * * * * *

Do not you see these afflicted persons & hear them accuse

you?—The Lord knows I have not hurt them.   I am an innocent person.

It is very awful for all to see these agonies and you an old professor, thus charged with contracting with the devil by the effects of it, and yet to see you stand with dry eyes when there are so many wet.—You do not know my heart.

You would do well if you are guilty to confess and give glory to God.—I am as clear as the child unborn.

What uncertainty there may be in apparitions I know not, yet this with me strikes hard upon you, that you are at this very present charged with familiar spirits, this is your bodily person they speak to. They say now they see these familiar spirits come to your bodily person, now what do you say to that?—I have none, sir.

Possibly you may apprehend you are no witch, but have you not been led aside by temptations that way?—I have not.

Tell us, have you not had vissible appearances more than what is common in nature?—I have none nor never had in my life.

Do you think these suffer voluntary or involuntary?—I cannot tell.

That is strange, every one can judge.—I must be silent.

They accuse you of hurting them & if you think it is not unwillingly but by design you must look upon them as murderers.—I cannot tell what to think of it.

Afterwards when this was somewhat insisted on she said, I do not think so. She did not understand aright what was said.

Well, then, give an answer now, do you think these suffer against their wills or not? I do not think these suffer against their wills.

Why did you never visit these afflicted persons?—Because I was afraid I should have fits too.

Upon motion of her body fits followed upon the complainants abundantly and very frequently.

Is it not an unaccountable case that when you are examined these persons are afflicted?—I have got nobody to look to but God.

Again upon stirring her hands the afflicted persons were seized with violent fits of torture.

Do you believe these afflicted persons are bewitched?—I do think they are.

When this witchcraft came upon the stage there was no suspicion of Tituba (Mr. Parris' Indian woman), she professed much love to that child, Betty Parris, but it was her apparition did the mischief, and why should not you also, be guilty, for your apparition doth hurt also?—Would you have me belie myself?

She held her neck on one side and accordingly so were the afflicted taken.

Then authority requiring it, Sam. Parris read what he had in characters taken from Mr. Thomas Putnam's wife in her fits.

What do you think of this?—I cannot help it, the devil may appear in my shape.

This is a true account of the sum of her examination, but by reason of great noises by the afflicted and many speakers many things are pretermitted memorandum.

Nurse held her head on one side and Elizabeth Hubbard (one of the sufferers) had her neck set in that posture, whereupon another patient, Abigail Williams, cried out, set up Goody Nurse's head, the maid's neck will be broke, and when some set up Nurse's head Aaron Way observed that Betty Hubbard's was immediately righted.

Salem Village, March 24th 169½ The Rev. Samuel Parris being desired to take in writing the examination of Rebecca Nurse hath returned it as aforesaid and seeing what we then did see together with the charge of the persons then present we committed Rebecca Nurse, the wife of Francis Nurse, of Salem Village unto their majesties' goal in Salem as per a mittimus then given out in order to further examination.

John Hathorne,
Jonathan Corwin, asts.

Goody Nurse remained in jail until the first of June, when she was brought before the grand

jury.   On June 2 the jury returned four indictments against her.   The first was for afflicting
Ann Putnam on March 24; the second and third
for afflicting Mary Walcott and Elizabeth Hubbard on the same day, and the fourth charged
her with afflicting Abigail Williams.   It will be
noticed that the date of the offences alleged in
these several indictments is that of the day of
the preliminary examination.   The same   is
noticeable in most of these witchcraft cases.   In
few of the indictments is the same date of offence alleged as in the original complaint before
the justices.   The witnesses in the case were
summoned to be present on Thursday, June 2 ;
the testimonies of Ann Putnam, Mary Walcott
and others against Nurse are dated and sworn to
June 2 and 3, and the indictments bear the same
date.   The court convened again on June 28
and there is on the files a " petition on behalf of
Rebecca Nurse " presented to the court " now
sitting in Salem."   It would seem that the trial
must have been delayed from the 3rd to the
28th.   At the trial which followed, Ann Putnam
deposed that on the 13th of March she

" Saw the apparition of Goody Nurse, and she did immediately afflict me, but I did not know what her name was
then, though I knew where she used to sit in our meeting
house, but since that she hath grievously afflicted by
biting, pinching and pricking me, and urging me to write
in her book and also on the fourth day of March, being the
day of her examination, I was grievously tortured by her

during the time of her examination, and also several times since, and also during the time of her examination I saw the apparition of Rebecca Nurse go and hurt the bodys of Mercy Lewis, Mary Walcott, Elizabeth Hubbard and Abigail Williams."

The deposition of Mary Walcott was in about the same language as the above, save that the apparition of Rebecca Nurse would kill her if she did not write in the book, and that Nurse "told her she had a hand in the death of Benjamin Houlton, John Harwood, Rebecca Shepard and several others." She saw the apparition of Goody Nurse during her examination go and hurt the bodies of Ann Putnam, Mercy Lewis, Elizabeth Hubbard and Abigail Williams. The depositions of Elizabeth Hubbard and Abigail Williams differed but little in tenor or in language from the above. Williams claimed to have been afflicted by Nurse on March 15, 16, 20, 21, 23, 31, and also on several days in May. Nurse had tempted her to leap into the fire, and she had "seen the apparition of a sacrament sitting next to [the man] with a high crowned hat." It had also confessed to her "its guilt in committing several murders together with her sister Cloys." The testimony of Sarah Vibber appears to have been given later in the month, for she deposed to being pinched and choked by the apparition of Rebecca Nurse on June 27. Among the other depositions in the case are the following:

The deposition of Johannah Childin [Sheldon] testifieth
and saith that ypon the 2nd of June, 1692, that the aperi-
tion of Goody Nuss and Goodman Harwood did apeare to
her and the said Harwood did look Goody Nuss in the face
and said to her that she did murder him by pushing him off
the cart and strock the breath out of his body."

Edward Putnam deposed that "on March 26 Ann Putnam, sen., was bitten by Rebecca Nurs as she said did,
about 2 of the clock the same day she was strock with a
chane the mark being in a band of a round ring and three
stroaks across the ring she had six blos with a chane in the
space of half an ower, and she had one remarkable one
with six stroakes across her arme.   I saw the mark both of
bite and chane."

Sarah Holten's deposition is the only paper
among all those on file that gives any information that Rebecca Nurse ever had trouble with
her neighbors or ever was called a railer and
brawler.   Perhaps in this case, allowance should
be made for the possible exaggeration of an
angry and excited neighbor.   The widow
Houlton deposed as follows :

About this time three years ago my dear & loving husband, Benjamin Houlten, deceased, was as well as ever I
knew him in my life, till one Saturday morning that Rebecca Nurse who now stands charged for witchcraft came
to our house and fell railing at him because our pigs got
into her field, tho our pigs were sufficiently yoked and
their fence was down in several places, yet all we could say
to her could no ways pacify her but she continued railing
and scolding for a great while, calling to her son Benj.
Nurse to go and get a gun and kill our pigs and let none of
them go out of the field, though my poor husband gave her
never a misbeholding word, and within a short time after
this my poor husband, going out very early in the morning,
as he was coming in again he was taken with a strange fit

in the entry being struck blind and struck down two or
three times so that when he came to himself he told me he
thought he should never have come into the house any
more, and all summer after he continued in a languishing
condition, being much pained at his stomach and often
struck blind, but about a fortnight before he died he was
taken with strange and violent fits acting much like to
our poor beloved parsons [persons] when we thought they
would have died and the doctor that was with him could
not find what his distemper was, and the day before he died
he was chearly, but about midnight he was again most
violently seized upon with violent fits till the next night
about midnight, he departed this life by a cruel death.

The following depositions found on the court
files indicate that there were those who dared to
testify in behalf of the accused. I quote both
exactly as they appear in the originals :

John Tarbell being at the house of Thomas Putnam
upon the 28th day of this instant March, being the year
1692, upon discourse of many things I asked them some
questions and among others I asked this question whether
the garle that was afflicted did first speak of Goody Nurse
before others mentioned her to her, they said she told them
she saw the apparishtion of a pale-fast woman that sat in
her gran-mother's seat but did not know her name, then I
replied and said, but who was it that told her that it was
Good Nurs ; Mercy Lewis said it was Goody Putnam that
said it was Goody Nurs ; Goody Putnam said it was Mercy
Lewes that told her ; thus they turned it upon one another,
saying it was you and it was you that told her, this was
before any was afflicted at Thoms Putnam's beside his
daughter, that they told his daughter it was Goody Nurs.
Samuel Nurs doth testifie too all above written.

We whos names are underwritten cane testifie if cald to
it that Goodde Nurs have beene troubled with an infirmity
of body for many years which the juries of women seem to

be afraid it should be somthing else Rbcah Preson, Mary
Tarbel.

This last statement refers to the witch mark
alleged to have been found on the body of Rebecca Nurse. One of the theories of the age
was that the devil set his mark upon each of
his servants ; that witches were all marked. A
jury of the sex of the accused was appointed to
examine the body for such marks. It often
happened that some excresence of flesh common
to old people, or one explainable by natural
causes, was found. One such had been found
on the body of Goody Nurse, and reported to
the court, all but one of the jury agreeing to the
report. Rebecca Preston and Mary Tarbell
knew that the mark was from natural causes.
The prisoner stated to the court that the dissenting woman of the jury of examination was
one of the most ancient, skilful and prudent,
and further declared, " I there rendered a sufficient known reason of the moving cause
thereof." She asked for the appointment of
another jury to inquire into the case and examine the marks found on her person. No documents have been found to indicate whether her
request was granted. Probably it was not.

The jury of trials returned a verdict of not
guilty on June 28. Thereupon all the accusers
in court " cried out " with renewed vigor and
were taken in the most violent fits, rolling and

tumbling about, creating a scene of the wildest confusion. The judges told the jurymen that they had not carefully considered one expression of the prisoner, namely, that when one, Hobbs, a confessing witch, was brought in as evidence against her she said : " What, do you bring her ? She is one of us." The jury retired for further consultation.[2] Even then they could not agree upon a verdict of guilty. They returned to the court room and desired that the accused explain the remark. She made no response and the jury returned a verdict of guilty.[3] On being informed that her silence had been construed as a confession of guilt, the prisoner made this statement :

These presence do humbly show to the honored court and jury, that I being informed that the jury brought me in guilty upon my saying that Goodwife Hobbs and her daughter were of our company; but I intended no otherwise than as they were prisoners with us, and therefore did then, and yet do judge them not legal evidence against their fellow prisoners: and I being something hard of hearing, and full of grief, none informing me how the court took up my words, and therefore had not an opportunity to declare what I intended when I said they were of our company.

Grave charges have been made against the chief justice in this case by some writers, to the effect that he fairly forced the jury to go out after the verdict of not guilty and that he practically told them to reverse the verdict.

2 Neal's New England, II., 143 ; Calef, Fowler's Ed. 251.

[Fac-Simile of page of Examination of Rebecca Nurse.]

The Examination
of Rebekah Nurse at Salem village
24th Mar. 1691/2

Mr. Hathorn - What do you say (speaking to one afflicted) have
you seen this woman hurt you?
Yes, she beat me this morning
Abigail Have you been hurt by this woman?
Yes

Ann Putnam in a grievous fit cryed out that
the said Nurse.
Goody Nurse here are two Ann Putnam the child &
Abigail williams complains of your hurting them
what do you say to it

N: I can say before my Eternal father I am innocent, &
God will clear my innocency

you do know whither you are guilty. I have familiarity
with the Devil, & now when you are here present to
see such a thing, as they testify a black man whispering in your ear, & God about you what do you say
to it.

It is all false I am clear

H. it not an unaccountable case that when they
you are examined these persons are afflicted a
I have got my body to look to God God

John Hathorne Assist

Jonathan Corwin

Thomas Fisk, one of the jurymen, made a statement a few days after the trial, in which he says, the court " objected to the verdict," and " manifested dissatisfaction," and " several of the jury declared themselves desirous to go out again and thereupon the court gave leave." He further stated that he " could not tell how to take the words in question till she had further opportunity to put her sense upon them ; " that going into court and mentioning the words and she making no reply nor interpretation of them, " whereupon these words were to me a principal evidence against her."[3]

It is plain from all the evidence upon this point that had the court as counsel for the accused, which it was then in the theory of the law, guarded her interests, Rebecca Nurse would not have been convicted. The question propounded to her by the jury would have been so explained that she could understand and answer it. After conviction she was sentenced to be hanged. The Governor granted a reprieve. Thereupon, she was excommunicated from the church, as the following from the records of the First Church in Salem will show :

1692. July 3. After sacrament, the elders propounded to the church—and it was by unanimous vote consented to

3 Fisk quoted the exclamation thus: " What, do these persons give in evidence against me now? They used to come among us." This differs very materially from the words quoted above from Neal and Calef.

— that our sister Nurse, being a convicted witch by the court, and condemned to die, should be excommunicated; which was accordingly done in the afternoon, she being present.

Upham says this was meant to be understood as an eternal doom.[4] People in those days looked upon excommunication from the church as expulsion from Heaven. What then must have been the feelings of this woman as she stood in the presence of her almost life-long church, a church which she loved, and to which she had been true and loyal for more than half a century, with the chains of a condemned witch clanking about her withered and tottering limbs, and heard the awful doom of her soul pronounced?[5] Happily the age of superstition is passed, and we know that wherever the noblest and best of mankind and womankind abide there rests the soul of this saint and martyr.

Immediately on the reprieve being granted the afflicted renewed their clamors. They claimed to be again grievously afflicted. Their renewed complaints, the action of the church at Salem, and the clamors of "some Salem gentleman" influenced the Governor to recall the re-

4 Salem Witchcraft, II., 291.
5 The sentence of excommunication was erased from the church book about 1712.

prieve and approve the sentence. Rebecca Nurse
was, therefore, on July 19, carted to the summit
of Gallows hill and hanged.

"They hanged this weary woman there,
  Like any felon stout;
Her white hairs on the cruel rope
  Were scattered all about."[6]

6 " The Death of Goody Nurse," by Rose Terry Cooke.

SARAH HOLTEN HOUSE, DANVERS.

CHAPTER VII.

REV. GEORGE BURROUGHS.

N speaking of Rev. George Burroughs, it seems proper to allude briefly to the early history of the Salem Village church. The witchcraft prosecutions have some times been attributed to the feelings engendered by the disagreements over the settlement of a pastor of the parish. Up to 1671 the people of Salem Villlage worshiped with the mother church in Salem. On March 22 of that year (1672 O. S.) the town of Salem voted that the farmers at the Village should "have liberty to have a minister by themselves, and when they should provide and pay him in a maintenance they should be discharged from their part of the Salem minister's maintenance."[1] Rev. James Bayley became "supply" minister of the parish in Nov. 1672, and a meeting house was erected in 1673. Some dissatisfaction was manifested with the manner of his call. The feeling increasing in intensity,

[1] Salem Town Records; Hanson's Hist. Danvers, 223.

an appeal was made to the parent church in Salem. Among Bayley's opponents were Nathaniel Putnam and Bray Wilkins, men of wealth and influence in the community. The dispute finally reached the General Court. That body decided in favor of the minister, and ordered that he be continued and settled, and be allowed £60 per annum, one-third in money and two-thirds in provisions and fuel for his family.[2] The people of the parish paid no attention to this order, and in 1679 Mr. Bayley resigned. Bayley came to the Village from Newbury, where he had married Mary Carr. His wife's sister, Ann Carr, accompanied them to Salem Village where, in 1678, she married Sergt. Thomas Putnam,[3] of whom we shall hear much before we have finished this story. This united the minister's family with the wealthiest and most powerful family in the place.

George Burroughs was engaged as preacher in place of Mr. Bayley in November, 1680. Graduating from Harvard in 1670, he early went into the district of Maine to preach, and dwelt for some time at Casco, now Portland, where he received a grant of 150 acres of land in a section now the very heart of the city. This land he generously gave to the town in later years. Mr. Burroughs early encountered hostility in his new

2 Rice's Hist. First Parish in Danvers, 15.
3 Savage's Genealogical Dictionary.

parish in Danvers, as was quite natural, from the partisans of his predecessor. His salary was not promptly paid, and when, in 1681, his wife died, he had no money to pay the funeral expenses. A violent dispute raged in the parish between the Bayley and anti-Bayley factions, and Burroughs gave up the pastorate in 1682. Even this did not end his troubles. He came back from Maine, whither he had moved, to "get a reckoning" or settlement, and was arrested for a debt due to John Putnam. Yet on the very day of his arrest he had signed an order for the payment to Thomas Putnam of the amount due to himself from the parish. It appears by a bill on file on the records that when Burroughs' wife died, John Putnam allowed him to buy two gallons of Canary rum, some cloth and other articles on his account. The debt was for less than £14, and the parish owed Burroughs £33 6s. 8d., so that Putnam was amply secured.[4]

Rev. Deodat Lawson succeeded Mr. Burroughs, coming to the Village in 1684. He found much discord prevailing, not only over the settlements of Bayley and Burroughs but also over the parish records, which it was alleged had not been correctly kept during their ministries. Both disputes were referred to members of the church in Salem for advice. The advice

[4] Salem Witchcraft, II., 262.

given was that certain changes be made in the records. Harmony could not be secured, however, and Mr. Lawson withdrew in 1688. Following him came Rev. Samuel Parris, who was ordained on Monday, Nov. 19, 1689. It is evident, therefore, that from the calling of Mr. Bayley in 1672 to the ordination of Mr. Parris in 1689 there was wanting in the parish that harmony so essential to church prosperity. That the disagreements about the settlements of the different pastors and over the parish records affected the minds of the people after the witchcraft delusion appeared among them there is little doubt. That it was the cause of the first charges being made seems hardly probable.

George Burroughs, on leaving Salem Village, returned to Casco, Maine. He remained there a long time, for he and others were there in 1690 when the settlement was raided by Indians. Burroughs then went to Wells, Maine, and preached a year or more. There he was living in peace and quietness when the messenger from Portsmouth came to arrest him, at the demand of the Salem magistrates, in 1692. After leaving Salem Village he had married a third wife, a woman who had been previously married and had children of her own ; for after Burroughs' death, when the Massachusetts colony granted compensation to his family, his children complained that this third Mrs. Burroughs took the

entire amount for herself and her children.[5] Mr.
Burroughs was a small, black-haired, dark com-
plexioned man, of quick passions and possessing
great strength.[6] We shall see by the testimony
to be quoted further on that most of the evidence against him consisted of marvellous tales
of his great feats of strength. We are told
that, "his power of muscle discovered itself
early when Burroughs was a member of Cambridge college, which fact convinces us that he
lifted the gun and the barrel of molasses by the
power of his own well-strung muscle and not by
any help of the devil."[7] Sullivan, in his History
of Maine, says that Burroughs was a man of
bad character and cruel disposition.[8] Fowler
declared that his researches lead him to a different conclusion.[7] Increase Mather wrote that
the testimony "proved him a very ill man,'"[7]
and confirmed the belief of the character which
had been already fastened on him. Cotton
Mather says in his account that "his tergiversa-
tions, contradictions and falsehoods were very
sensible at his examination and on his trial."
Hutchinson says of Burroughs' trial, that "he
was confounded and used many twistings and
turnings, which I think we cannot wonder at."[9]

5 Essex Court Records.
6 Putnam's Salem Witchcraft Explained, 278.
7 Calef's "More Wonders, etc." Fowler's ed., 278-290.
8 p. 209.   9 Hist. Mass., II., 39.

All these statements appear to be founded, more
or less, on Cotton Mather's "Wonders of the
Invisible World." Unfortunately we have none
of the testimony offered for the defence, if any
there was. Possibly there was none. Mr.
Burroughs was nearly a hundred miles distant
from the places where he had lived much of his
time, and far from his friends. He was among
a people largely hostile, and perhaps was denied
all opportunity to obtain friendly witnesses.
Whatever we may say about the trials being
conducted according to the English law, which
did not then allow counsel to the accused,
but in theory considered the judges his counsel,
it is undeniable that in this case, as in many other of these witchcraft trials, the interests of the
accused were not properly guarded. The whole
conduct of the judges, from beginning to end,
was that of prosecuting attorneys. Preconceived
belief in the guilt of the accused is evidenced
throughout by their acts and by their words.

The only ground of explanation, and that by
no means satisfactory, and certainly not a justi-
fication, is that the court was following the
advice given to Major Richards by Cotton
Mather, that "whatever hath a tendency to put
the witches into confusion is likely to bring
them unto confession too. Here crosse & swift
questions have their use." . . "A credible
confession of the guilty wretches is one of the

most hopeful ways " he says, " of coming at them, & I say a credible confession, because even confession itselfe sometimes is not credible. . . I am far from urging the un-English method of torture " to obtain confessions.[10]

The warrant for the arrest of George Burroughs was issued in Portsmouth, N. H., on April 30, 1692, by " Elisha Hutchinson, major," directed to Jno. Partridge, " field marshal," requiring him to " apprehend the body of Mr. George Burroughs at present preacher at Wells, in the Province of Maine and convey him with all speed to Salem, . . he being suspected for a confederacy with the devil in oppressing of sundry about Salem, as they relate," he (Hutchinson) having received " particular order from the governor and council of their majesties colony of the Massachusetts for the same." Partridge returned that by virtue of the warrant he " had apprehended said George Burroughs and have brought him to Salem and delivered him to the authority there this fourth day of May, 1692."[11]

Some question has been raised about the haste with which the arrest was made. The warrant was issued on the last day of April. On May 2, Hutchinson addressed a letter to Hathorne and Corwin, saying he had " caused Burroughs to be apprehended and sent to Salem." This

10 Mass. Hist. Coll., VIII., 391.   11 Ibd., V., 32.

letter Partridge probably took to Salem with him on that day. This would give him two days to go to Wells and return to Portsmouth, and the third and fourth in which to reach Salem. The time was ample, even in those days of slow travel. Depositions charging Burroughs with being concerned in the witchcraft business had been made as early as April 23. After formal complaint had been made and the warrant issued, it was natural that matters connected with the arrest should be expedited. Burroughs remained in jail until the 9th of May, when he was examined. Stoughton and Sewall come down to assist Hathorne and Corwin in the work. A private inquiry was instituted by the judges and the ministers of the neighboring churches. The record of that portion of the examination is as follows :

Being asked when he partook of the Lord's supper, he being (as he said) in full communion at Roxbury, he answered it was so long since he could not tell, yet he owned he was at meeting one Sabbath at Boston, part of the day, and the other at Charlestown part of a Sabbath when the sacrament happened to be at both yet did not partake of either. He denied that his house at Casco was haunted yet he owned there were toads. The above was in private none of the bewitched being present.

Then followed the examination in open court :

At his entry into the court room many (if not all of the bewitched) were grievously tortured. Susan Sheldon testified that Burroughs' two wives appeared in their winding sheets and said that man killed them. He was bid to look upon Susan Sheldon. He looked back and knocked down all (or most of the afflicted who stood behind him.)

Mercy Lewis' deposition going to be read and he looked at her and she fell into a dreadful and tedious fit.

Mary Walcott,	Testimony going to
Elizabeth Hubbard,	be read and they
Susan Sheldon,	all fell into fits.

Being asked what he thought of these things he answered it was an amazing and humiliating providence but he understood nothing of it, and he said (some of you may observe that) when they begin to name any name they cannot name it . . . . The bewitched were so tortured that authority ordered them to be taken away some of them.

Capt. Putnam testified about the gun. Capt. Wormwood testified about the gun and the molasses.

He (Burroughs) denied that about the molasses. About the gun he said he took it before the lock and rested it upon his breast.

John Brown testified about a barrel of cider.

He denied that his family was affrighted by a white calf in his house.

I have quoted thus much of the examination, not because the testimony is important, but that the reader may understand the nature of the evidence introduced in these witchcraft trials. Burroughs was committed to prison by the magistrates, and remained there until August, when he was indicted and tried. Four indictments were found against him. One charged him with afflicting Mary Walcott, a second with afflicting Elizabeth Hubbard, the third with afflicting Mercy Lewis, and the fourth, Ann Putnam. Neal, who wrote about 1747, says

Burroughs was brought upon his trial on August 5.

Among the more interesting depositions made during the trial of Burroughs were those of Ann Putnam and Mercy Lewis, two of the afflicted. Ann testified that Burroughs appeared to her one night and told her he had had three wives and had bewitched the two first of them to death. Subsequently, she testified that Burroughs' two first wives appeared to her when Mr. Burroughs was present; that they turned their faces towards Burroughs and "looked very red and angry," and told him that he had been a very cruel man to them; that they should "be clothed with white robes in heaven when he should be cast into hell." As soon as Burroughs disappeared the two turned their faces toward Ann, "and looked as pail as a white wall," and told her they were his two first wives and that he had murdered them. "One told me," she continues, "she was his first wife and he stabbed her under the left arm and put a piece of sealing wax on the wound, and she pulled aside the winding sheet and showed me the place." The second wife told Ann, "that wife which he hath now, killed her in the vessel as she was coming to see his friends."

In reading this remarkable piece of evidence, which is given here substantially in the language of the original, it is important not to lose sight of the fact that Ann Putnam, the reputed author of it, was only twelve years of age. Are we not forced to one of two conclusions : either that the girl's story is literally true, or that it was manufactured for her by her father or some other of the older people interested in the prosecution ? Would a girl of that age be capable of "manufacturing" such a story ? To whom shall we attribute the authorship ? To Thomas Putnam ? If he manufactured this, how much more of the witchcraft testimony owes its origin to the same source ? I am not disposed to sit in judgment in this matter ; but certainly even the casual reader should not be allowed to fill his mind with these remarkable statements without having his attention called to important controlling facts.

The statement of Mercy Lewis is equally remarkable. She deposed that on the night of May 9, Burroughs carried her up on to a high mountain and showed her " all the kingdoms of the earth and told me that he would give them all to me if I would write in his book, and if I would not he would throw me down and break my neck." She told him she would not write in the book if he threw her down on "100 pitchforks."

A great portion of the testimony against
Burroughs, as I have said, consisted of statements regarding his phenomenal strength.
Samuel Webber, for instance, told how Mr.
Burroughs put his finger into the bung of a
barrel of molasses lifted it up and carried it
around him and set it down. This is the only
direct testimony of great feats of strength
which does not discredit itself. No doubt this is
an exaggeration of the facts or a misapprehen-
sion of the circumstances. Thomas Greenslit's
testimony which is given below is the only
other direct evidence of phenomenal strength.
Everything else is hearsay evidence. As for
Greenslit, he appears to have been a man utterly
devoid of character, and not to be believed.
His deposition bears date September 15, which
would be nearly a month after the execution of
Burroughs. May it not have been procured
after the execution, to offset the indignation of
some of Burroughs' friends ?

We may as well dispose of Greenslit at this
point, by giving the substance of his deposition,
although not in chronological order. He deposed that he saw Mr. Burroughs, who was
lately executed,

" lift a gun of six foot barrel or thereabouts putting the
forefinger of his right hand into the muzzell of said gun
and that he held it out at arms end only with that finger,
and further this deponent testifieth that at the same time
he saw the said Burroughs take a full barrel of molasses

with but two of fingers of one of his hands and carry it from the stage head to the end of the stage.''

Simon Willard testified to being in Falmouth, Me., in September, 1689, when some one was

"commending Mr. Burroughs, his strength, saying that he could hold out his gun with one hand. Mr. Burroughs being there said, I held my hand here behind the lock and took it up and held it out. I, said deponent, saw Mr. Burroughs put his hand on the gun, to show us how he held it and where he held his hand, and saying there he held his hand when he held his gun out; but I saw him not hold it out then. Said gun was about seven foot barrel and very heavy. I then tried to hold out said gun with both hands but could not do it long enough to take sight.''

Willard also deposed that when he was in garrison at Saco some one in speaking of Burroughs' great strength said he could take a barrel out of a canoe and carry it and set it on the shore, and Burroughs said he had " carried a barrel of molasses or cider and that it had like to have done him a displeasure, so he intimated that he did not want strength to do it but the disadvantage of the shore was such that his foot slipping in the sand he had liked to have strained his leg.'' Benjamin Hutchinson testified that he met Abigail Williams one day about 11 o'clock in the forenoon, in Salem Village. Burroughs was then in Maine, a hundred miles away. She told him she then saw Burroughs. Hutchinson asked where. She answered, " there," and pointed to a rut in the road. Hutchinson threw an iron fork towards

the place where she said she saw Burroughs.
Williams fell into a fit.

Coming out she said, "You have torn his coat for I heard
it tear." "Whereabouts? said I." "On one side said
she." Then we went to the house of Lieut. Ingersoll, and
I went into a great room and Abigail came in and said,
"there he stands." I said, "where? where?" and presently drew my rapier. Then Abigail said "he is gone but
there is a gray cat." Then I said "whereabouts?"
"There," said she, "there." Then I struck with my
rapier and she fell into a fit; and when it was over she
said, "you killed her."

Hutchinson said he could not see the cat,
whereupon Williams informed his credulous
soul that the spectre of Sarah Good had come
in and carried away the dead animal.

These affairs, be it remembered, occurred in
broad day-light. Deliverance Hobbs, called as
a witness in the case, protested her innocence.
Subsequently she was examined in prison and
confessed that she was a witch. She had attended a meeting of witches where Burroughs
was preacher, and "pressed them to bewitch all
in the village. He administered the sacrament
to them with red bread and red wine like blood.
. . . Her daughter, Abagail Hobbs, being
brought in at the same time, while her mother
was present, was immediately taken with a
dreadful fit; and her mother being asked who
it was that hurt her daughter, answered it was
Goodman Corey, and she saw him and the

gentle woman of Boston striving to break her daughter's neck."

I quote at this point a deposition exactly as I find it on the files, without the change of a letter or a punctuation mark. Besides being a good illustration of the evidence relied upon to convict persons of witchcraft, it gives an insight into the intellectual condition of a portion of the people of the day :

The complaint of Samuel Sheldon against Mr. Burroughs which brought a book to mee and told mee if i would not set my hand too it hee would tear me to peesses i told him i would not then he told mee hee would Starve me to death then the next morning hee tould me hee could not starve mee to death but hee would choake mee so that my vittals should doe me but litl good then he tould mee his name was borros which had preached at the yilage the last night hee came to mee and asked mee whither i would goe to the village to morrow to witness against him i asked him if he was examined then he told mee hee was then i told him i would goe then hee told mee hee would kil me before morning then hee apeared to mee at the house of nathanniel ingolson and told mee hee had been the death of three children at the eastward and had kiled two of his wifes the first he smothered and the second he choaked and killed two of his own children.

Ann Putnam, it will be remembered, told an entirely different story about the way in which Burroughs " killed his two first wives," and she claimed to have the story directly from the apparitions of those wives.

A jury of seven appointed to search the body of Mr. Burroughs for witch marks reported that they found nothing but what was natural.   He was convicted, however, and on the 19th of August hanged on Gallows hill, Salem.

Calef says he was "carried in a cart with the others through the streets of Salem to execution. When he was upon the ladder he made a speech for the clearing of his in-nocency with such solemn and serious expressions as were to the admiration of all present: his prayer which he con-cluded by repeating the Lord's prayer so well worded and uttered with such composedness and such (at least seeming) fervency of spirit, as was very affecting, and drew tears from many, so that it seemed to some that the spectators would hinder the execution. The accusers said the black man stood and dictated to him.[14] As soon as he was turned off, Mr. Cotton Mather, being mounted upon a horse, addressed himself to the people, partly to declare that he (Burroughs) was no ordained minister, and partly to possess the people of his guilt saying that the devil has often been transformed into an angel of light; and this somewhat ap-peased the people and the execution went on. When he was cut down, he was dragged by the halter to a hole, or grave, between the rocks, about two feet deep, his shirt and breeches being pulled off, and an old pair of trowsers of one executed put on his lower parts. He was so put in together with Willard and Carrier that one of his hands and his chin, and a foot of one of them, were left uncovered."[15]

Judge Sewall wrote under date of August 19 :

"This day George Burroughs, John Willard, John Proc-ter, Martha Carrier and George Jacobs were executed at

14 A person guilty of witchcraft was supposed to be incapa-ble of repeating the Lord's prayer correctly, although this was only incidental and corroborative testimony and was never considered as in any sense conclusive. It is not certain that the repetition was always demanded by the magistrates or judges. It does appear however that the accused often voluntarily re-peated the prayer as Burroughs did on this occasion.

15 Fowler's Ed., 254.

Salem, a very great number of spectators being present, Mr. Cotton Mather was there, Mr. Sims, Hale, Noyes, Cheever &c. All of them said they were innocent, Carrier and all. Mr. Mather says they all died by a Righteous Sentence. Mr. Burrough by his Speech, Prayer, presentation of his Innocence did much move unthinking persons, which occasions their speaking hardly concerning his being executed."[16]

Thus ended the life of the most important personage executed during this period and one of the most noted of witchcraft victims in the history of the world. Whatever opinions we may entertain with regard to the general subject of witchcraft, or of the mistakes of the courts in these cases, only one opinion seems possible concerning the treatment of the accused before and after trial. They were treated with the grossest brutality, from the beginning to the end, from the most aged and infirm to the youngest and most innocent.

16 Sewall Papers, 369.

CHAPTER VIII.

BRIDGET BISHOP AND THE JACOBS FAMILY.

RIDGET Bishop was arrested April 19, 1692, on a warrant issued the day before. Her examination took place on the day of arrest, and she was committed to jail. Bridget was the second wife of Edward Bishop, "sawyer." Bishop was her third husband. Her first was one Wasslebee, and her second, Thomas Oliver. Bishop himself married again nine months after Bridget was hanged. The Bishops at the time of Bridget's arrest were living near the line between Salem Village and Beverly, on the road which now leads from North Beverly to Danversport, and nearly opposite the Cherry hill farm. Goodwife Bishop kept some sort of a public house for the entertainment of travelers. From the documents on file it appears that she sold cider, if nothing stronger, and that her guests sat up late at night playing at shovelboard, drinking and making so much noise that the neighbors complained of the place. Bishop and his first wife Hannah, were before the court

in 1653 and fined, he for " pilfering of apples "
and lying, and she for stealing Indian corn and
lying.[1] Bishop was also fined for contempt of
court in not obeying a summons in January,
1692. Bridget Bishop was arrested on a charge
of witchcraft in 1680, tried and discharged. It
is evident, therefore, that neither of them stood
before the community in the best possible light.
Any new charge to the discredit of either was
quite likely to be believed.

Samuel Gray, who preferred the charge of
witchcraft against this woman in 1680, testified
long after, on his death bed, his sorrow and repentance for such accusations as being wholly
groundless.[2] The court reporter on the occasion
of Bridget Bishop's examination before the
magistrates in 1692 left this record :

As soon as she came near all fell into fits.

Mary Walcott said that her brother Jonathan stroke her
appearance and she saw that he had tore her coat in striking and she heard it tear. Upon some search in the court a
rent that seems to answer what was alleged was found.

They say you bewitched your first husband to death.—If
it please your worship, I know nothing of it.

She shake her head and the afflicted were tortured.

The like again upon motion of her head.

The court sought to make her confess by leading questions repeated in various forms, but
was unable to shake her firm denial of every
charge.

1 Essex County Court at Ipswich, 1653, Nos. 42-43.
2 Calef, Fowler's ed., 247.

The report continues :

Then she turned up her eyes and the eyes of the afflicted were turned up.

It may be you do not know that any have confessed to-day who have been examined before you that they are witches.—No, I know nothing of it. John Hutchinson and John Lewis in open court affirmed that they had told her.

Why, look you, you are taken now in a flat lie.—I did not hear them.

The remainder of the report is so nearly like that in other cases that its use here would be mere repetition. The prisoner was sent to jail. The new court of Oyer and Terminer, which had been constituted by Gov. Phips on May 27, sat in Salem, June 2, for the trial of Bridget Bishop, Rebecca Nurse and others. She was, therefore, one of the first persons tried by the new court, and one of the first of the alleged witches of Salem and Salem Village to be tried in 1692. The evidence against her at this trial has come down to us with a considerable degree of fulness. There were five indictments. They charged the prisoner in the usual form with witchcraft in, upon and against Mercy Lewis, Abigail Williams, Mary Walcott, Elizabeth Hubbard and Ann Putnam, respectively. In addition to the customary testimony of the af-flicted that the shape of the accused did often pinch, bite, choke and otherwise hurt them, and had urged them to write their names in a book, which the apparition called "our book," they manifested the usual evidences of torture in the court room. Among the interesting testimony in the case was that of William Stacey, who deposed that he had the small pox some thirteen years before, and Bridget Bishop professed great love for him in his affliction. Some time after he did some work for her, for which she paid him three pence. He put the money in his pocket ; but had not gone above three or four rods when he looked in his pocket but could not find any money. One day he met Bishop going to mill ; she asked him whether his father would grind her grist. He wished to know why she asked. She answered, because folks counted her a witch.

"Deponent made answer he did not doubt his father would grind it, but being gone about six rods from her with a small load in his cart, suddenly the off wheel plumped or sunk down into a hole upon plain ground, that this deponent was forced to get one to help him get the wheel out. Afterwards he went back to look for said hole where his wheel sunk in, but could not find any hole."

One winter about midnight he felt something cold pressing on his teeth between his lips. He saw "Bishop sitting on the foot of the bed." She "hopt upon the bed and about the room." Some time after, Stacey,

"In a dark night, was going to the barn, who was suddenly taken or hoisted from the ground, threw against a stone wall, after that taken up again and throwed down a bank at the end of the house. Some time after this deponent met the said Bridget Bishop by Isaac Stone's brick kill; after he had passed by this deponent's horse stood still with a small load going up hill, so that the horse trying to draw, all his gears flew in pieces and the cart fell down."

Rev. John Hale of Beverly, testified that the wife of John Trask desired of him that Bishop be not permitted to receive the Lord's Supper till she had given satisfaction for some offences

TRASK HOUSE, NORTH BEVERLY.

that were against her because she " did entertain certain people in her house at unseasonable hours in the night to keep drinking and playing at shovel-board whereby discord did arise in the other families and young people were in danger to be corrupted." He greatly feared that " if a stop had not been put to those disorders Edward

Bishop's house would have been a house of great prophainness and iniquity." The next news he heard of Christian Trask was that she was "distracted," and her husband said she was so taken the night after she complained of Goody Bishop. He continued his testimony at length, stating that the "distractions returned from time to time until Mrs. Trask died. As to the wounds that she died of I did observe three deadly ones, a piece of her windpipe cut out, another wound above it through the wind pipe and gullets the veins they call juglar, so that I then judged and still do apprehend it impossible for her with so short a pair of scissors to mangle herself so without some extraordinary work of the devil or witchcraft." Is there any reason to doubt, after reading this testimony, that Christian Trask was insane, and so committed suicide?

Two witnesses testified that on taking down the cellar wall in the old Bishop house where Bridget lived in 1685, they found in holes in the wall several poppits made up of rags and hog's brussels with headless pins in them with the points out. Poppits were believed to represent the person whom the witch desired to afflict, and by sticking pins into those images the mischief was supposed to be mysteriously and safely accomplished. Whatever was done to the images was, so the belief ran, done to the person whom they represented.[3]

Samuel Shattuck testified that Bridget Bishop came to his house to buy a hogshead which he asked very little for, and she went away without it. Sundry other times she came in a smooth flattering manner he had thought since to make mischief. At or very near this time his eldest child which had promised much health and understanding was "taken in a drooping condition and as she came often to the house it grew worse and worse. As he would be standing at the door would fall out and bruise his face upon a great step-stone as if he had been thrust out by an invisible hand." Sometimes the child would go out in the garden and get on a board and when they would call it it would walk to the end of the board and hold out its hands as if it could come no further and they had to lift it off. Again, Bishop brought him a pair of sleeves to dye. He dyed them and she paid him two pence. He gave the money to Henry Williams, and Williams told him he put it in a purse among some other money and put the purse in a box and locked the box. He never after found the money or purse in the box. "It had gone out." John Lander testified that Bishop came into his room one night and sat on his stomach. He put

3 Essex Inst. Hist. Coll., II., 143.

out his hands and she grabbed him by the throat and choked him. One Sunday while he remained at home :

"The door being shut I did see a black pig in the room coming towards me, so I went towards it to kick it and it vanished away. Immediately after I sat down in a narrow bar and did see a black thing jump into the window and came and stood just before my face upon the bar, and the body of it looked like a munkey and I being greatly affrighted, not being able to speak or help myself by reason of fear I suppose, so the thing spake to me and said, I am a messenger sent to you for I understand you are troubled in mind, and if you will be ruled by me you shall want for nothing in this world, upon which I endeavored to clap my hands upon it, and said you devil I will kill you, but could feel no substance and it jumped out of the window again, and immediately came in by the porch although the doors were shut, and said you had better take my council, whereupon I strooke at it with a stick but struck the ground-sill. Then his arm was disennabled, and opening the door and going out he saw Bishop in her orchard going towards her house, and seeing her had no power to set one foot before the other."

Another piece of testimony against Bridget Bishop was that of John Bly and wife. They had a dispute with the Bishops about a hog. They testified that the hog was taken with "strange fits, jumping up and knocking her head against the fence, and seemed blind and deaf, and would not eat, neither let her pigs suck but foamed at the mouth." They gave it red ochre and milk which made it better but soon "it did set off jumping and running as if she was stark mad, and, after that was well again, and we did then apprehend or judge and do still, that said Bishop had bewitched said sow." John Cook told the court that five or six years previously he was assaulted with the shape of the prisoner in his chamber, and so terrified that an apple that he had in his hand flew strangely from him into his mother's lap six or eight feet distant.

The trial occupièd most of the week. Bridget was convicted and sentenced to be hanged. She was executed on Friday, June 10, being the only person hanged on that day, and hence the first victim of the great witchcraft delusion of 1692. Calef says, " she made not the least confession of anything relating to witchcraft."[4] Of her execution we have no details, but the court records contain the original warrant for her execution and the sheriff's return thereon. As this is the only death warrant which has been preserved in these cases it is quoted here in full :

To George Corwin gentᵐ High Sheriff of the county of Essex greeting:

Whereas Bridget Bishop, als Oliver, the wife of Edward Bishop of Salem in the county of Essex, sawyer, at a speciall court of Oyer and Terminer held at Salem the second day of this instant month of June for the countyes of Essex, Middlesex and Suffolk before William Stoughton Esq. and his associate justices of the said court was indicted and arraigned upon five several indictments for using, practicing and exercising on the nynteenth day of April last past and divers other days and times before and after

4 Fowler's Ed., 247.

certain acts of witchcraft on and upon the bodyes of Abigail Williams Ann Putnam junr. Mercy Lewis May Walcott and Elizabeth Hubbard of Salem Village single women
whereby their bodyes were hurt afflicted pined consumed
wasted and tormented contrary to the forme of the statute
in that case made and provided. To which indictment the
said Bridget Bishop pleaded not guilty and for tryal thereof
put herself upon God and her country whereupon she
was found guilty of the felonyes and witchcraft whereof she

BRIDGET BISHOP HOUSE, NORTH BEVERLY.

stood indicted and sentence of death accordingly passed agt
her as the law directs. Execution whereof yet remains to
be done. These are therefore in the name of their maj(es)-
ties William and Mary now King and Queen over England
&c to will and command you that upon Fryday next being
the tenth dy of this instant month of June between the
hours of eight and twelve in the aforenoon of the same day
you safely conduct the sd Bridget Bishop als Oliver from
their majties goal in Salem aforesd to the place of execu-

tion and there cause her to be hanged by the neck until she be dead, and of your doings herein make return to the clerke of the sd court and pr cept. and hereof you are not to faile at your peril and this shall be your sufficient warrant given under my hand and seal at Boston the eighth dy of June in the fourth year of the reign of our Sovirgne Lord & Lady William & Mary now King and Queen over England &c annogr dom 1692

William Stoughton

According to the within written precept I have taken the body of the within name[d] Brigett Bishop out of their majesties goal in Salem and safely conveighed her to the place provided for her execution and caused ye sd Brigett to be hanged by the neck untill she was dead [and buried in the place] all which was according to the time within required and so I make returne by me.

George Corwin Sheriff.

The words in brackets in the sheriff's return were written in the original and then partially erased. They are important, however, as indicating the disposition of Bishop's body. No doubt other bodies were disposed of in the same manner. Corwin probably erased the words after writing them because the matter of burial was not mentioned in the warrant.

The history of the Jacobs family in connection with the witchcraft prosecutions is peculiarly interesting. George Jacobs, Sen., George Jacobs, Jun., and his wife Rebecca and daughter Margaret, were all accused. The old man must have been seventy years of age or more, for he had long, flowing white hair. He lived on a farm in what was then known as Northfields, and in Salem rather than Salem Village, but on territory now included in the town of Danvers. The exact site was near the mouth of Endicott or Cow House river, the first of the three rivers one crosses in driving from Salem to Danvers. Jacobs was evidently a man of some property, and probably a good average citizen; but, like most of the others who fell under suspicion of witchcraft, and for that matter, many of their neighbors, he had had a little trouble which had brought him into court. The records show that in 1677 he was fined for striking a man. His son, George, jun., three years earlier, was sued by Nathaniel Putnam to recover the value of some horses that he had chased into the river where they were drowned. The court found against Jacobs.[5] On the 10th day of May, 1692, Hathorne and Corwin issued a warrant "to the constable of Salem" directing him to apprehend George Jacobs, sen., of Salem, and Margaret Jacobs, daughter of George Jacobs, jun., of Salem, single woman. On the same day, Joseph Neal, "constable for Salem," returned that he had apprehended the bodies of George Jacobs, sen., and Margaret Jacobs. They

5 George Jacobs, jun., being complained of for driving of horses into the river and threatening to drown them and some horses lost and one found dead in the river shortly afterwards the court . . . . found the said Jacobs blamable and that they do adjudge him to pay the charge arising upon the hearing of the case, the costs is 20s. County Court, Salem, I, No. 11.

were taken to Salem that day, and the examination of the old man was begun at once. After
some preliminary questions and the usual " sufferings " of the afflicted, the report continues,
Jacobs saying:

BEADLE TAVERN, SALEM.

I am as innocent as the child born to-night. I have lived
33 years here in Salem.

What then?—If you can prove that I am guilty I will lye
under it.

Sarah Churchill said, last night I was afflicted at Deacon
Ingersoll's, and Mary Walcott said, it was a man with 2
staves. It was my master.

Pray do not accuse me. I am as clear as your worships You must do right judgements.

What book did he bring you, Sarah?—The same book that the other woman brought.

The devil can go in any shape.

Did he not appear on the other side of the river and hurt you? Did not you see him?—Yes, he did.

Look there, she accuseth you to your face, she chargeth you that you hurt her twice. Is it not true?—What would you have me say? I never wronged no man in word nor deed.

Here are 3 evidences.—You tax me for a wizzard. You may as well tax me for a buzzard. I have done no harm.

Is it not harm to afflict these?—I never did it.

But how comes it to be in your appearance?—The devil can take any license.

Not without their consent.—Please your worships, it is untrue, I never showed the book. I am silly about these things as the child born last night.

That is your saying. You argue you have lived so long, but what then, Cain might (have) live so long before he killed Abel and you might live long before the devil had so prevailed on you.—Christ hath suffered 3 times for me.

What three times?—He suffered the cross and gal . .

You had as good confess (said Sarah Churchill) if you are guilty.

Have you heard that I have any witchcraft?

I know that you lead a wicked life.

Let her make it out.

Doth he ever pray in his family?

Not unless by himself.

Why do you not pray in your family?—I cannot read.

Well you may pray for all that. Can you say the Lord's prayer? Let us hear you.

He might [missed] in several parts of it & could not repeat it right after many trials.

Sarah Churchill, when you wrote in the book you was showed your master's name you said—Yes sirr.

* * * * * * * * * *

Well, burn me or hang me I will stand in the truth of Christ. I know nothing of it.

This examination, begun on the 10th, was suspended for some reason before completion, and finished on the 11th. On that day the accusing girls were present in full force. Among them was Sarah Churchill, who gave very positive evidence against the prisoner. Subsequently, Sarah Ingersoll deposed.—

That seeing Sarah Churchill after her examination, she came to me crying, and wringing her hands, seemingly much troubled in spirit. I asked her what ailed her. She answered she had undone herself. I asked in what. She said in belying herself and others in saying she had set her hand to the devil's book whereas she said I never did. I told her I believed she had set her hand to the book. She answered and said, no, no, no. I never did. I asked her then what made her say she did. She answered because they threatened her, and told her they would put her into the dungeon and put her along with Mr. Burroughs, and thus several times she followed me up and down telling me she had undone herself, in belying herself and others. I asked her why she did not deny she wrote it. She told me because she had stood out so long in it, that now she durst not. She said, also, that if she told Mr. Noyes but once she had set her hand to the book, he would believe her, but if she told the truth, and said she had not set her hand to the book a hundred times he would not believe her.

George Herrick testified that in May he went to the jail and searched the body of Jacobs. He found a tett under the right shoulder a quarter of an inch long. He ran a pin through it but "there was neither water, blood nor corruption, nor any other matter, and so we make return."

The following document is also among the papers :—

wee whose names are under written having received an order from ye sreife to search ye bodyes of George Burroughs and George Jacobs wee find nothing upon ye body of ye above sayd Burroughs but wt is naturall but upon ye body of George Jacobs wee find 3 tetts wch according to ye best of our judgements wee think is not naturall for wee run a pinn through 2 of ym and he was not sincible of it one of them being within his mouth upon ye inside of his right cheak and 2d upon his right shoulder blade and a 3d upon his right hipp.

Ed Welch sworne	John Flint jurat
Will Gill sworne	Tom West sworne
Zeb Gill jurat	Sam Morgan sworne
	John Bare jurat.

The jury found Jacobs guilty, and he was sentenced to the gallows, and executed on August 19.[6] After his condemnation the sheriff's officers went to his house and seized all his goods, and even took his wife's wedding ring. It was with great difficulty that she obtained it again. She was under the necessity of buying provisions of the sheriff, such as he had taken from her. These not being sufficient to sustain life, the neighbors supplied her with more.

In the mean time warrants were issued on May 14, for George Jacobs, jun., and his wife Rebecca. Jacobs escaped. When the constables took Rebecca she had four young children in her home. Some of them followed her on the road, but being too young to continue far they were left behind, and cared for by the neighbors. Rebecca Jacobs was kept in irons eight months, then indicted and brought

6 Jacobs was buried on his farm in Danversport, where his grave may be seen at this day. The remains were exhumed about 1864, examined and redeposited in the earth where they had lain for nearly two centuries. The skull was found to be fairly well preserved. The jaw bones were those of an old man, the teeth being all gone. A metalic pin was the only article found save the bones. Family tradition has it that Jacobs was hanged on a tree on his own farm. Mr. C. M. Endicott says his grandmother, a direct descendant, told him that the body after execution in Salem was brought home for burial by his son, who witnessed the hanging. Others say it was a grandson. Essex Inst. Hist. Coll., I., 53 Calef, Fowler's Ed., 258

GRAVE OF GEORGE JACOBS, DANVERSPORT, WITH JACOBS' HOUSE IN THE DISTANCE.

to trial on January 3, 1693. She was promptly acquitted. In the mean time touching petitions had been presented to the chief justice by the mother, and to Gov. Phips, praying for her re. lease. They were of no avail. The woman was kept in a dungeon, half fed, and uncared for beyond what was necessary to sustain life, through the long winter months. Her treatment was in keeping with that of other victims. In cruelty and barbarity it must be frankly said that it finds parallel only in the acts of the savages of the forests. Whether the officials were actuated by honest motives in the prosecutions, may be a fair question, but there is no question that the treatment of prisoners was malignant and full of the spirit of persecution.

Margaret Jacobs, to save herself from punishment acknowledged that she was a witch and testified against her grandfather, and also against Mr. Burroughs. On August 2, 1692, the day after Mr. Burroughs and George Jacobs, sen., were executed, she addressed a letter to her father as follows :—

Honored father,—After my humble duty remembered to you, hoping in the Lord of your good health, as blessed be God I enjoy, though in abundance of affliction, being close confined here in a loathsome dungeon, the Lord look down in mercy upon me, not knowing how soon I shall be put to death, by means of the afflicted persons. My grandfather having suffered already and all his estate seized for the king. The reason of my confinement is this, I having, through the magistrates' threatenings, and my own vile and wretched heart, confessed several things contrary to my own conscience and knowledge, though to the wounding of my own soul, the Lord pardon me for it. But O, the terrors of a wounded conscience, who can bear? But blessed be the Lord, he would not let me go on in my sins, but in mercy, I hope, to my soul, would not suffer me to keep it in any longer, but I was forced to confess the truth of all before the magistrates, who would not believe me, but 'tis their pleasure to put me here, and God knows how soon I shall be put to death. Dear father, let me beg your prayers to the Lord on my behalf, and send us a joyful and happy meeting in Heaven. My mother, poor woman, is very crazy, and remembers her kind love to you, and to uncle, viz. d—A—, so leaving you to the protection of the Lord, I rest your dutiful daughter.

Margaret Jacobs.

From the dungeon
in Salem prison,
Aug. 20, 1692.

At the next session of the court Margaret made another confession in which she said,

"The Lord above knows I know nothing in the least measure, how or who afflicted them, they told me without doubt I did, or else they would not fall down at me, they told me if I would not confess I should be put down into the dungeon and would be hanged, but if I would confess I should have my life. The which did so affright me with my own vile wicked heart, to save my life made me make the like confession I did, which confession, may it please the honored court is altogether false and untrue. . . . Whatever I said was altogether false against my grandfather and Mr. Burroughs, which I did to save my life and to have my liberty, but the Lord, charging it to my conscience made me in so much horror that I could not contain myself before I had denied the confession, which I did, though I saw nothing but death before me, choosing rather death with a quiet conscience than to live in such horror, which I could not suffer. Whereupon my denying my confession I was committed to close prison."

She asked the court to take pity and compassion on her young and tender years, she having no friend but the Lord to plead her cause. At the time set for her trial she was troubled with a disorder in her head, and thus escaped. The evidence which she gives as to the pressure brought to bear to make her confess herself a witch corroborates what was said by many others, and raises the question in our minds whether all the so-called confessions were extorted by similar promises of mercy on the one hand, and threats of punishment on the other. Margaret remained in prison some time after the proclamation of freedom was issued by the governor, because she could not pay the fees and charges of the jailer.

CHAPTER IX.

THE PROCTERS, WILLARD, CARRIER AND HOW.

HE story of the trial of John Procter and his wife Elizabeth is full of interest. The Procters lived originally in Ipswich, but subsequently in Salem Village, at the point now known as Procter's Crossing in Peabody. The house stood near the southerly end of Pleasant hill. Procter was a respectable and well-to-do farmer. He came into conflict on one or two occasions with Giles Corey, but this does not seem to have had anything to do with the subsequent proceedings on the charge of witchcraft against him or his wife, although the same efforts have been made in this case as in many others to attribute the prosecution to personal animosities. Procter, in 1678, was a referee in a case between Corey and John Gloyd. The decision of Procter, and the other arbitrators was against Corey, but that did not appear to create any ill-feelings between the two, and they are said to have drunk together after the

decision had been announced.[1] A short
time after this Procter's house caught fire
and some one was unkind enough to suggest
that Corey set the fire, as already mentioned in
an earlier chapter. As there stated, he was acquitted, when brought to trial.

PROCTER HOUSE, PEABODY.

Complaint was made against Elizabeth Procter on April 4, by Capt. Jonathan Walcott and
Lieut. Nathaniel Ingersoll, for afflicting Abigail
Williams, John Indian, Mary Walcott, Ann
Putnam and Mercy Lewis. She was arrested on
the 11th, and taken to Salem for examination,
together with Sarah Cloyes, sister of Rebecca

1 Essex Court Records.

Nurse. Danforth, deputy governor, Samuel Appleton, Samuel Sewall and Isaac Addington sat with Hathorne and Corwin on this occasion. Procter himself, like a good husband, followed his wife to court, but at the cost of his life. The girls of the accusing circle cried out against him and he was then and there arrested. During the examination of Goodwife Procter, this scene occurred :

Elizabeth Procter, you understand whereof you are charged, viz., to be guilty of sundry acts of witchcraft. What say you to it? Speak the truth, and so you that are afflicted, you must speak the truth as you will answer for it before God another day. Mary Walcott, doth this woman hurt you?—I never saw her so as to be hurt by her.

Mercy Lewis, does she hurt you?—(Her mouth was stopped.)

Ann Putnam, does she hurt you?—(She could not speak.)

Abigail Williams, does she hurt you?—(Her hand was thrust in her own mouth.)

John Indian, does she hurt you?—This is the woman that came in her shift and choked me.

Did she ever bring the book?—Yes, sir.

What to do?—To write.

What, this woman?—Yes, sir.

Are you sure of it?—Yes, sir.

Again Abigail Williams and Ann Putnam were spoke to by the court, but neither of them could make any answer, by reason of dumbness, or other fits.

What do you say, Goody Procter, to these things?—I take God in Heaven to be my witness, that I know nothing of it, no more than the child unborn.

Ann Putnam, doth this woman hurt you?—Yes, sir, a great many times. (Then the accused looked upon them and they fell into fits).

*   *   *   *   *   *   *   *

Did not you, said Abigail, tell me that your maid had written?—Dear child it is not so. There is another judgement, dear child.

Then Abigail and Ann had fits. By and by they cried out, "Look you, there is Goody Procter on the beam." Shortly both of them cried out of Goodman Procter himself, and said he was a wizzard. Immediately many, if not all, the bewitched, had grievous fits.

Ann Putnam, who hurt you?—Goodman Procter and his wife.

Afterwards, some of the afflicted cried, there is Procter going to take up Mrs. Pope's feet, and her feet were immediately taken up.

What do you say, Goodman Procter, to these things?—I know not, I am innocent.

* * * * * * * *

During the examination of Elizabeth Procter, Abigail Williams and Ann Putnam both made offer to strike at said Procter but when Abigail's hand came near it opened —(whereas it was made up into a fist before) and came down exceeding lightly, as it drew near to said Procter and at length, with open and extended fingers, touched Procter's hood very lightly. Immediately, Abigail cried out, her fingers, her fingers, her fingers were burned.

The following document which was filed in the case of Procter and his wife and Sarah Cloyes, was the form used in all other cases. It is quoted here more for the light it throws on the methods of procedure in those days than for its importance in this or any other one case :

Salem, April 11th, 1692. Mr. Samuel Parris was desired by the Honorable Mr. Danforth, deputy governor, and the council, to take in writing the aforesaid examinations, and accordingly took and delivered them in, and upon hearing the same, and seeing what was then seen, together with the charge of the afflicted persons, were by the advice of the council all committed by us.

John Hathorne Ass't's.
Jonathan Corwin.

Procter and his wife were brought to trial about August 5. I find three indictments against him on the files. One charges that he afflicted Mary Walcott on April 11; a second that he afflicted Mercy Lewis on the same day, and the third that he afflicted Mary Warren on March 26. Two indictments against Elizabeth Procter are on file. One charges that she afflicted Mary Walcott, the other that she afflicted Mercy Lewis, the date of the offence alleged in each case being April 11. The testimony offered at these trials differed very little from that used to convict in other cases, and the witnesses were substantially the same. One or two of the depositions are of rather more than ordinary interest, perhaps. Among them, I find this somewhat remarkable production :

Elizabeth Booth testified that on ye 8th of June hugh joanes Apered unto me & told me that Elesebeth Prockter kiled him because he had a poght of sider of her which he had not paid her for. On June 8th Elesebeth Shaw Apered unto me & told me yt Elesebeth Procter & John Willard kiled Her Because she did not use those doctors she Advised her to. . . Ye wife of John Fuller Apered unto me and told me that Elesebeth Procter kiled her because she would not give her Áples when she sent for sum. . . . The apparition of Law Shapling and Doc Zerubabel Endicott appeared and said Elizabeth Procter killed them, and the apparition of Robert Stone, sen., told him that John Procter and his wife killed him, and at the same time Robert Stone, jr., appeared and said Procter and his wife killed him because he took his father's part.

John Bailey deposed that,

" On the 25th of May last myself and wife being bound to Boston on the road, when I came in sight of the house where John Procter did live there was a very hard blow struck on my breast, which caused great pain in my stomach and amazement in my head, but did see no person near me only my wife on my horse behind me on the same horse; and when I came against said Procter's house, according to my understanding, I did see John Procter and his wife at said house. Procter himself looked out of the window, and his wife did stand just without the door. I told my wife of it; and she did look that way and see nothing but a little maid at the door. Afterwards, about a mile from the aforesaid house, I was taken speechless for some short time. My wife did ask me several questions, and desired me if I could not speak I should hold up my hand; which I did and immediately I could speak as well as ever. And when we came to the way where Salem road cometh into Ipswich road, there I received another blow on my breast, which caused me so much pain I could not sit on my horse. And when I did alight off my horse, to my understanding, I saw a woman coming towards us about 16 or 20 pole from us, but did not know who it was. My wife could not see her. When I did get up on my horse again, to my understanding, there stood a cow where I saw the woman."

As matter of fact, Procter and his wife were at this time, in jail in Boston, and had been there since April 11. Bailey was undoubtedly frightened at the stories he had heard the previous evening in Salem Village, where he must have passed the night on his way from his home in Newbury to Boston. His wife, who perhaps had not heard the stories about Procter and other "witches," was not agitated and could plainly see that there was only a maid standing at the door. As for Bailey's other troubles that morning, we may believe as much or as little as we please of the story he told. We know now that there was not a particle of reality in it. It may have been deliberate falsehood, or it may have been the effect of a too fervid imagination. Of Procter's family, Benjamin, the oldest, was in prison with his parents ; and his sister Sarah, aged sixteen, William, aged eighteen, Samuel, aged seven, Abigail between three and four, and one still younger, were about home. William was sent to prison three days later, so it must have been the "little maid," Abigail, whom Bailey saw standing in the door way.

Daniel Elliott testified that he heard one of the accusing girls say that she cried out against Goodman Procter for sport. "The girls must have some sport," she is said to have added.[2]

Procter and his wife were convicted, and sentenced to be hanged. Every effort possible was made to save him from suffering the penalty. John Wise and thirty-one old neighbors in Ipswich signed a petition in his behalf to the court of assistants. They said :

"We reckon it within the duties of our charity, that teaches us to do as we would be done by, to offer thus much

2 Putnam's Salem Witchcraft Explained, 449.

for the clearing of our neighbors' innocency, viz., that we never had the least knowledge of such a nefandus wickedness in our neighbors since they have been within our acquaintance. . . . As to what we have ever seen or heard of them, upon our conscience we judge them innocent of the crime objected."

Nathaniel Felton and twenty of their nearer

NATHANIEL FELTON, JR. HOUSE.

Salem Village neighbors signed a similar petition, saying:

"We whose names are underwritten, having several years known John Procter and his wife do testify that we never heard or understood that they were ever suspected to be guilty of the crime now charged upon them, and several of us, being their near neighbors, do testify, that to our apprehension, they lived christian like in their family, and were ever ready to help such as stood in need of their help."

Procter wrote a letter to Rev. Messrs. Increase

Mather, Allen, Moody, Willard and Bailey, which was signed by himself and several of his fellow prisoners, in which he said :

"Here are five persons who have lately confessed themselves to be witches, and do accuse some of us of being along with them at a sacrament, since we were committed into close prison, which we know to be lies. two of the five are (Carrier's children) young men, who would not confess anything till they tied them neck and heels, till the blood was ready to come out of their noses. My son William Procter, because he would not confess that he was guilty when he was innocent, they tied him neck and heels till the blood gushed out at his nose."

This letter was written after the preliminary examinations, and while the prisoners were lying in jail awaiting trial. They asked that they might be tried in Boston, and if not, that they have other magistrates,—requests which show in the strongest manner that the trials were notoriously unfair, for no accused persons would take the risk of offending the magistrates before whom they might be tried unless the emergency was a most extraordinary one, because failure to attain the object sought was sure to be prejudicial to their cause. They also begged that some of the ministers be present at the trials, "hoping thereby you may be the means of saving the shedding of our innocent blood." No attention was paid to this appeal for fairness in trial, nor to the appeals for life subsequent to Procter's conviction and sentence. He was executed on August 19. His body, it is believed by his descendants, was recovered afterwards and buried on his farm, where it has since reposed.

Elizabeth Procter escaped by pleading pregnancy. Some months after the death of her husband she gave birth to a child.[3] Her home had been desolated. Not only had her husband been hanged, three of her children imprisoned, and she herself brought within the very shadow of the gallows, but the officers of the law had stripped that home of all its worldly possessions. Her execution was again ordered early in 1693, but Gov. Phips granted a reprieve. Many of her relatives in Lynn were accused and some brought to trial. All in all, the severe treatment of this family has led to the charge of special persecution. The reason for this, it is believed, was Procter's intense opposition to the witchcraft prosecutions from the very beginning, and particularly when he said he could " whip the devil out of them."[4] Possibly if he could have applied his remedy to the accusing girls, in the beginning, we should never have had any " Salem Village Witchcraft."

John Willard of Salem Farms was employed

---

[3] Savage's Genealogical Dictionary of New England gives the date Jan. 27, 1692-3; but the correctness of this is questioned.

[4] "Lieut. Ingersoll declared yt John Proctor tould Joseph Pope yt if he hade John Indian in his custody he would soon beat ye devill out of him, and so said severall others." Court Records, Salem.

during the earlier days of the witchcraft prosecutions to assist in bringing in persons accused. Accusations were finally made against Willard himself. It has been stated that he was charged because he had expressed sympathy with the accused and doubts of the justice of the proceedings. One remark quoted is : " Hang them, they are all witches." Just why this remark should bring upon him the displeasure of the prosecutors is not easy to understand. Is it not more probable that he was cried out against, as so many others were, from no apparent motive, but through the excitement and terror of the times? He was " talked about " for some time before any movement was made to arrest him. He went to his grandfather, Bray Wilkins, and asked the old man to pray with him, but Wilkins was just going from home and could not stop then. He told Willard he would not be unwilling if he got home before night, but Willard did not reappear. On election week Wilkins and his wife, both more than eighty years of age, rode to Boston on their horse. Willard went also with Henry Wilkins, jr. Daniel Wilkins, Henry's son, had heard the stories about Willard and protested against his father going with him. He is quoted as saying of Willard : " It were well if Willard were hanged." On election day, Bray Wilkins and his wife and Rev. Deodat Lawson were at Lieut. Richard Ways' house for

dinner. Willard and Henry Wilkins came in
later. The elder Wilkins says he thought Willard did not look on him kindly, for, he says,
" to my apprehension, he looked after such a
sort upon me as I never before discerned in
any." Wilkins was taken very sick that afternoon and remained so some days. He was carried home, and on arriving there, found Daniel
Wilkins, the young man who had advised his
father not to go to Boston with Willard, also
very ill. The old man himself fell ill again.
Mercy Lewis and Mary Walcott were sent for
to come and solve the mystery of so much sickness in the Wilkins family. They were, as
usual, equal to the occasion. They "saw the
apparitions of Sarah Buckley and John Willard
upon the throat and breast of Henry Wilkins,"
and saw them press and choke him until he
died. Lewis then went to the room where old
Bray Wilkins lay. Asked if she saw any thing,
she replied : " Yes, they are looking for John
Willard." A little later she exclaimed : " There
he is upon his grandfather's belly."

A warrant for Willard's arrest was issued on
May 10 on complaint of Thos. Fuller and others.
Two days later, Constable Putnam returned the
document with the endorsement that he had
made search for him and could not find him. He
was produced in court on the 18th, having been
arrested in Groton. Among the more interest-

ing papers on file in the case is the following
deposition of Mrs. Ann Putnam. Whether it
was presented to the magistrates to induce them
to issue a warrant for Willard's arrest, or was
given in at the preliminary examination   at

SITE OF BEADLE TAVERN, ESSEX STREET, SALEM, MASS.

Beadle's tavern in Salem, we have no means of
knowing. The document is as follows :

The shape of Samuel Fuller and Lydia Wilkins this day
told me at my own house by the bedside, who appeared in
winding sheets, that if I did not go and tell Mr. Hathorne
that John Willard had murdered them they would tear me
to pieces. . . . At the same time the apparition of John

Willard told me that he had killed Samuel Fuller, Lydia Wilkins, Goody Shaw and Fuller's second wife, and Aaron Way's child, and Ben Fuller's child and this deponent's child, Sarah, six weeks old, and Phillip Knight's child with the help of William Hobbs, and Jonathan Knight's child and two of Ezekiel Cheever's children with the help of William Hobbs; and Elliott and Isaac Nichols

BENJAMIN FULLER HOUSE, MIDDLETON.
[His child bewitched to death by Willard.]

with the help of William Hobbs. . . . Joseph Fuler's apparition also the same day came to me and told me that Goody Corey had killed him.

Must we not accept one of two explanations of this remarkable piece of evidence : that the whole story was literally true, and therefore witchcraft a reality, or that Mrs. Ann Putnam deliberately falsified? Will the theory of general terror and hallucination in the community sufficiently explain the statement? Were the people " out of their wits", as Martha Carrier said? On the other hand, I am bound to say that I find no evidence of any cause which should prompt Mrs. Putnam to make such serious charges against Willard and others, unless we accept the claim of some writers who profess to believe that it was for the purpose of supporting the general plan of prosecution for witchcraft. Willard was committed to jail, and subsequently tried at the August session of the court. Only one piece of evidence has been preserved from this trial. Susan Sheldon, eighteen years of age, testified that at Nathaniel Ingersoll's house, on May 9, she saw the apparitions of four persons.—

William Shaw's first wife, the widow Cook, Goodman Jones and his child, and among these came the apparition of John Willard to whom these four said, you have murdered us. These four having said thus to Willard they turned as red as blood. And turning about to look at me they turned as pale as death. These four desired me to tell Mr. Hathorne. Willard hearing them, pulled out a knife, saying if I did he would cut my throat." . . . On another occasion there came to her a shining man and told her to go and tell Hathorne. She told him she would if he would hunt Willard away, she would believe what he said. "With that the shining man held up his hands and Willard vanished away. About two hours after, the same appeared to me again and the said Willard with them, and I asked them where their wounds were and they said there would come an angel from Heaven and would show them, and forthwith the angel came. . . . And the angel lifted up his winding sheet, and out of his left side he pulled a pitchfork-tine and put it in again, and likewise he opened all the winding sheets and showed all the wounds. And the white man told me to tell Mr. Hathorne of it and I told him to hunt Willard away, and I would, and he held up his hand, and he vanished away." She also saw Willard suckle the apparitions of two black pigs on his breasts.

THOMAS FULLER HOUSE, MIDDLETON.
[Fuller was a complainant against Willard.]

John Willard was found guilty and sentenced to be hanged; and on August 19 he was executed. Brattle says of Willard and Procter at their execution, that " their whole management of themselves from the jail to the gallows was very affecting, and melting to the hearts of some considerable spectators."[5]

5 Mass. Hist. Coll., I., V., 68.

Martha Carrier was arrested, probably on May 28, as the warrant against her was issued on that day. She was examined on the 31st. Martha was about forty years of age, and the mother of a large family of children, four of whom were taken into custody at the same time that she was. We have little information regarding her life previous to her arrest. At the examination before the local magistrates they said to her: " You see you look upon them and they fall down." " It is false," she replied ; " the devil is a liar. I looked upon none since I came into the room but you." Susan Sheldon said: " I wonder what could you murder thirteen persons for." Goodwife Carrier repelled the insinuation, and the afflicted all had terrible fits. She charged that the magistrates were unfair, and said : " It is a shameful thing that you should mind these folks that are out of their wits." To the accusers she cried : " You lie, I am wronged." The recorder of the trial adds :

" The tortures of the afflicted were so great that there was no enduring it, so that she was ordered away and to be bound hand and foot with all expedition, the afflicted in the meanwhile almost killed. As soon as she was well bound they all had strange and sudden cease."

Martha Carrier was committed to prison where she remained until the August term of court, when she was tried, convicted and sentenced. Her execution took place on the 19th of the same month.

Her daughter Sarah, eight years of age, confessed herself a witch and testified against her
mother.   Little Sarah said she had been a witch
since she was six years old, that her mother
made her a witch and made her set her hand to
the book.   The place where she did it was in
Andrew Foster's pasture.   The witches promised
to give her a black dog, but it never came to her.
A cat came to her and said it would tear her in
pieces if she would not set her hand to the
book.   Her mother came like a black cat.   The
cat told her that she was her mother.   Richard
Carrier, eighteen years of age, told the magistrates that he had " been in the devil's snare."
His examination continued as follows :

Is your brother Andrew ensnared by the devil's snare?—
Yes.

How long has your brother been a witch?—Near a month.

How long have you been a witch?—Not long.

Have you joined in afflicting the afflicted persons?—Yes.

You helped to hurt Timothy Swan, did you?—Yes.

How long have you been a witch?—About five weeks.

Who was at the Village meeting when you were there?—
Goodwife How, Goodwife Nurse, Goodwife Wilds, Procter
and his wife, Mrs. Bradbury and Corey's wife.

What did they do there?—Eat, and drink wine.

From whence had you your wine?—From Salem, I think.

Goodwife Oliver there?—Yes, I know her.

During the trial of Martha Carrier, Benjamin
Abbott testified that he had some land granted
to him by the town of Andover, and,—

" When this land came to be laid out Goodwife Carrier
was very angry, and said she would stick as close to Benja-

min Abbott as the bark stuck to a tree, and that I should
repent of it before seven years came to an end, and that
Dr. Prescott could never cure me. These words were also
heard by Allen Toothaker. She also said to Ralph Farnum,
jr., that she would hold my nose so close to the grind stone
as ever it was held since my name was Benjamin Abbott.
Presently after I was taken with a swelling in my foot, and
then was taken with a pain in my side, exceedingly tormented, which led to a sore which was lanced by Dr. Prescott, and several gallons of corruption did run out, as was
judged." This continued six weeks and subsequently he
had two sores in the groin which brought him almost to
death's door and continued, " until Goodwife Carrier was
taken and carried away by the constable, and that very day
I began to grow better," therefore he had great cause to
think that Carrier had a great hand in his sickness. Abbott's wife testified to all the above, and also that there was
" terrible sickness and death among the cows, some of
whom would come up out of the woods with their tongues
hanging out of their mouths in a strange, affrighting manner."

The case of Elizabeth How, wife of James
How, husbandman, sometimes described as of
Ipswich and sometimes as of Topsfield, has always excited much interest. The documents in
the case show that she was a woman of most
exemplary character, devout and pious, kind and
charitable. These traits availed her nothing,
however, when children accused her of witchcraft. She was arrested on May 29, on a warrant issued the previous day, and brought before
the magistrates for examination on the 31st.
Elizabeth How was torn from a loving and afflicted husband and two interesting daughters.

Her husband was blind, and it is related that after his wife was placed in Salem jail he and one daughter used to ride thither twice each week to visit her. After the conviction and sentence, one of the devoted daughters went to Boston to beg for the life of her mother, but the governor was immovable. On her being brought before the magistrates, the girls went through their usual performances. " What say you to this charge?" asked Hathorne. " If it was the last moment I was to live," she replied, " God knows I am innocent of anything in this nature." She was committed for trial, and tried at the sitting of the court in July. The first charge against her was made by a Perley girl ten years of age. There had been trouble between the How and Perley families, which is pretty clearly stated in the testimony that follows. Timothy Perley and his wife Deborah testified that,—

There being some difference between Goode How and Timothy Perley about some boards, the night following three of our cows lay out, and finding them the next morning we went to milk them and one of them did not give but two or three spoons fuls of milk and one of the other cows did not give above a half a pint, and the other gave a quart, and these cows used to give three or four quarts at a meale; two of these cows continued to give little or nothing four or five meals and yet they went in a good English pasture, and within four days the cows gave their full proportion of milk that they used to give.

These witnesses further deposed that Elizabeth How—

" Afflicted and tortured their daughter, ten years of age, until she pined away to skin and bone and ended her sorrowful life."   Also that How desired to join the church in Ipswich and they went there to testify against her and " within a few days after had a cow well in the morning as far as we know, this cow was taken strangely running about like a mad thing a little while and then ran into a great pond and drowned herself, and as soon as she was dead my sons and myself towed her to the shore and she stunk so that we had much ado to slea her."

Francis Lane testified that he helped James How get out some posts and rails, and How's wife told them she did not think the posts and rails would do, because John Perley helped get them, and when they went to deliver the posts and rails the ends of some forty broke off, although Lane said, " that in his apprehension they were good sound rails."   Capt. John How, brother-in-law of Elizabeth, testified that she asked him to go with her to Salem Farms, when she was to be examined, and he declined because he had to go to Ipswich, and that soon after he got home,

" Standing at my own door talking with one of my neighbors, I had a sow with six smale pigs in the yard, the sow was as well as far as I know as ever one, a sudden she leaped up about three or four feet high and turned about and gave one squeak and fell down dead."

He told his neighbor he thought the animal was bewitched, and then cut off her ear, and the hand he had the knife in was " so numb and full of pain that night and several days after that I could not do any work, and I suspected no other

person but my said sister Elizabeth How."
Samuel Phillips and Mr. Payson, minister of
Rowley, went one day to see this ten years old
daughter of the Perleys, and she told Goodwife
How in their presence that " if she did complain
of her in her fits she did not know that she did
so." They also affirmed that a brother of the
girl, looking out of a chamber window, told her
to say that Goodwife How was a witch, and
" the girl spake not a word." Elizabeth How
was hanged with others on Tuesday, July 19.

CHAPTER X.

SUSANNA MARTIN, MARY EASTY AND OTHERS.

USANNA Martin of Amesbury was a widow. She had been charged with witchcraft as early as 1669, but escaped conviction at that time. Her examination in 1692 took place at the Village on May 2, the warrant having been issued on the 30th of April. In the preliminary examination, Goodwife Martin was confronted by about the same witnesses and the same sort of testimony as those who had preceded her. The following extract from the record of her examination is interesting :—

Hath this woman hurt you?—Abigail Williams declared that she had hurt her often. Ann Putnam threw her glove at her in a fit. And the rest were struck dumb at her presence.

What, do you laugh at it?—Well I may at such folly.

* * * * *

What ails these people?—I do not know.

But what do you think ails them?—I do not desire to spend my judgement upon it.

Do you think they are bewitched?—No, I do not think they are.

Well tell us your thoughts about them.—My thoughts are mine own when they are in, but when they are out they are another's.

* * * * *

Do you believe these afflicted persons do not say true?—
They may lie for aught I know.

May not you lie?—I dare not tell a lie if it would save
my life.

Who do you think is their master?—If they be dealing in
the black art you may know as well as I.

The afflicted complained that they were
piuched and saw her on the beam. Then the
magistrates said: "Pray God discover you if
you be guilty." Martin replied: "Amen, amen.
A false tongue will never make a guilty person."
Then there was an uproar in the room. The
girls had terrible fits and John Indian shouted:
"She bites, she bites." All the girls pretended
to be struck down when they approached her.
Martin was committed to jail, where she remained until the 29th of June when she was
brought before the higher court for trial. At
her trial one singular piece of testimony was
offered. It was evidence of such peculiar neat-
ness on the part of Goodwife Martin as to lead
a neighbor to conclude that she was a witch.
This neighbor testified that Susanna Martin
came to her house in Newbury one very stormy
day in an "extraordinary dirty season," when it
was not fit for any person to travel. She asked
her if she came from Amesbury afoot, and expressed surprise thereat, and told her children
to give Mrs. Martin a chance to get to the fire
and dry herself. Martin replied, "she was as
dry as I was, and I could not perceive that the

soles of her shoes were wet." This, the witness declared, startled her and she at once concluded that the woman was a witch.

John Kembal deposed that he agreed to purchase a puppy from Martin, but not keeping his bargain, and purchasing a puppy from some one else, she remarked she would " give him puppies enough." Coming from his intended's house soon after sunset one night,

"There did arise a little black cloud in the north-west and a few drops of rain and the wind blew hard. In going between John Weed's house and the meeting house there did appear a little thing like a puppy of a darkish color. It shot between my legs forward and backward." He used all possible endeavors to cut it with his axe, but could not hurt it, and as he was thus laboring with his axe, the puppy gave a little jump from him and seemed to go into the ground. "In a little further going there did appear a black puppy somewhat bigger than the first but as black as a coal," to his apprehension, which came against him "with such violence as its quick motions did exceed the motions of his axe," do what he could. And it flew at his belly, and away, and then at his throat and over his shoulder one way, and off and up at it again another way, and with such violence did it assault him as if it would tear out his throat or his belly. He testified that he was much frightened but recovered himself and ran to the fence, "and calling upon God and naming the name of Jesus Christ, and then it invisibly flew away."

Barnard Peach deposed that Susanna Martin, " six or seven years past," came in at his window, took hold of his feet and drew his body into a heap and lay upon him for an hour and a half or two hours ; finally he put out his hand

and taking hold of hers drew it up to his mouth
and bit three of her fingers to the breaking of
the bones. Several other depositions of similar
character to these were given in at the trial,
and Susanna Martin was found guilty and executed on July 19.

Mary Easty, wife of Isaac Easty of Topsfield,
and sister of Rebecca Nurse and Sarah Cloyse,
was fifty-eight years of age in 1692, and the
mother of seven children. The Eastys lived on,
and owned one of the largest farms in the town.
It was the farm known to the present generation
as the Peirce farm, having for many years been
owned by Col. Thomas W. Peirce, and occupied
by him as a summer residence until his death in
1885. Previous to the ownership of Col. Peirce
the proprietor was Mr. B. W. Crowninshield. A
warrant for the arrest of Mary Easty was issued
by the magistrates on April 21, and she was examined on the following day and committed to
prison. During her examination, the magistrates
said to her : " Confess if you be guilty ; " to
which she replied : " I will say it, if it was my
last time, I am clear of this sin." Her answers
to this and other questions had evidently led the
magistrates to have doubts as to her guilt, for
they asked the accusing girls if they were certain this was the woman, and they all went into
fits. Subsequently they said : " O, Goody Easty,
Goody Easty, you are the woman, you are the

woman." On May 18, for reasons which the present age knows not nor ever can know, Mary Easty was released. Two days after her discharge, Mercy Lewis, living at Constable John Putnam's, had a fit and performed in a manner usual to the accusing girls. A messenger was sent for Ann Putnam to come and tell who afflicted Mercy. At Ann's home he found Abigail Williams, and the girls visited Mercy Lewis and declared that they saw Mary Easty and John Willard afflicting her body.[1] John Putnam and Benjamin Hutchinson went to Salem the night of the 20th of May and procured from Hathorne a warrant for the arrest of Mrs. Easty. She was apprehended the next morning and taken to Beadle's in Salem for examination.

"After midnight, she was aroused from sleep by the unfeeling marshal, torn from her husband and children, carried back to prison, loaded with chains, and finally consigned to a dreadful and most cruel death. She was an excellent and pious matron. Her husband, referring to the transaction nearly twenty years afterwards justly expressed what all must feel, that it was 'a hellish molestation.'"[2]

For the second time Mary Easty was examined and committed to jail. She remained there from May 21 until the September sitting of the court, when she was tried, convicted and sentenced. Previous to the trial, she united with her sister, Sarah Cloyse, in a request to the court that the judges would act as counsel for

1 Essex Court Papers.   2 Salem Witchcraft, II., 205.

them and direct them wherein they stood in need. This request to the judges after several trials had been held would indicate that such service was not being rendered to the accused persons. That this was the fact we have already seen in other cases. Instead of acting as counsel for the prisoners, the judges usually performed more nearly the part of prosecuting attorneys, and cross-examined the accused, often in a brow-beating manner. These sisters also asked that witnesses in their behalf might be examined. They especially named the pastor and others of the church in Topsfield. If those persons previously tried had been allowed their rights in this particular, why did Mary Easty and Sarah Cloyse petition thus to the court? After conviction, and while in jail awaiting execution, Mary Easty petitioned the Governor, judges and ministers,

"Not for my own life, for I know I must die, and my appointed time is set, but the Lord he knows it is that, if it be possible, no more innocent blood may be shed, which undoubtedly cannot be avoided in the way and course you go in. . . . By my own innocency, I know you are in the wrong. . . . I would humbly beg of you that your honors would be pleased to examine these afflicted persons strictly, and keep them apart some time, and likewise to try some of these confessing witches, I being confident there is several of them has belied themselves and others, as will appear, if not in this world, I am sure in the world to come whither I am now agoing."

Sarah Cloyse who was convicted and sentenced

at the same time, was never executed. No
record or tradition remains to tell us why she
was saved from the slaughter. Hutchinson
says, speaking generally of the seven persons
sentenced at this time, but not executed :—
" Those who were condemned and not executed,
I suppose all confessed their guilt. I have seen
the confessions of several of them."[3] Mary
Easty was hung on Thursday, September 22.
"When she took her last farewell of her husband, children and friends she was," says
Calef, " as is reported by them present, as
serious, religious, distinct and affectionate as
could well be expressed, drawing tears from the
eyes of all present."[4]

Of Alice Parker, Mary Parker, Wilmot Reed,
Margaret Scott, Ann Pudeator and Sarah Wildes
not much that is new can be said. The documents which have come down to us in their
cases are less voluminous than those in many
others. What record we have indicates that
theirs was the old, old story. Their accusers
were the same as in other cases. The testimony
was substantially the same. The conduct of the
accusers and the treatment of the prisoners by
the court and the officers of the law differed
only in detail from that in the cases already so
fully explained in the preceding pages.

Alice Parker of Salem was wife of John Par-

3 Hist. Mass., II., 59.   4 Fowler's Ed., 261.

ker, mariner. She was arrested on a warrant
dated May 12, examined before the local magistrates and committed to jail. Her trial took
place in September. She was convicted, together with Mary Parker, Wilmot Reed, Margaret
Scott and Ann Pudeator. All were executed on
Thursday, the 22d. One piece of evidence in
the case of Alice Parker is somewhat amusing,
read at this distance from the tragic event with
which it was connected. Jonathan Westgate
testified that Parker came to Beadle's tavern
one night and scolded her husband for drinking
so much there. Westgate took the part of the
husband. Mrs. Parker called him a rogue, told
him he had better mind his business, and that
he had better said nothing. Some time after
this, as he was going home one night, a black
hog appeared to him running at him with open
mouth. He endeavored to get away from it but
fell down. He said he fell on his hip, and his
knife run into his hip. When he got home his
knife was still in the sheath, and when he took
it out the sheath fell to pieces. His stockings
and shoes were full of blood, and he had to
crawl along by holding to the fence. The hog
he apprehended was either the devil or some evil
thing, not a real hog. He " did then really
judge or determine in his mind that it was either Goody Parker or by her means and procuring,
fearing that she is a witch." I presume that

all who read this story will conclude that Westgate was drunk that night, that when he fell his
knife-point went through the end of the sheath
and cut him, and at the same time the sheath
was cut open or crushed. When he got up,
Westgate was probably so drunk that he could
not walk without holding on to the fence.

Mary Parker was of Andover, and a widow.
A warrant for her arrest was issued on September 1, being one of the latest issued for any person who was subsequently executed. She was
examined on the following day before Hathorne,
Corwin, Gedney and Higginson, "justices of the
peace." She was charged with practicing witchcraft on Martha Sprague of Boxford. Samuel
Shattuck at the trial testified that one time a
man took her up to carry her home,

"But in a little way going he let her fall upon a place of
stones, which did not awake her, which caused me to think
she was really dead, after that we carried her into the
house and caused her clothes to be taken off, and while we
were taking off her clothes to put her into bed she was up
and laughed in our faces."

Jonathan Bullock testified to seeing Parker
lying out in the dirt and snow. Mary Wardwell
"owned she had seen the shape of Parker when
she afflicted Swan and Martha Sprague, but did
not know Parker was a witch."

Ann Pudeator, widow of Jacob Pudeator, was
about seventy years of age. She was arrested
on Thursday, May 12, on charge of witchcraft,

and examined the same day. She appears to
have been discharged and rearrested about July
2, for on that day she was again examined. She
was committed to jail and remained there until
tried at the September sitting of the court and
convicted. We have no particulars of her execution save that it occurred on Thursday, September 22. After sentence Mrs. Pudeator addressed a petition to the court in which she
declared that the

"Evidence of Jno. Best, sr., and Jno. Best, jr., and
Samuel Pickworth, which was given against me in court,
were all of them altogether false and untrue, and, besides,
the aforesaid Jno. Best hath been formerly whipped and
likewise is recorded for a liar."

Ann Pudeator was the mother of the notorious
Thomas Greenslitt who testified to the herculean
feats performed, or alleged to have been performed, by Mr. Burroughs. She owned some
property in Salem.

Wilmot Reed was wife of Samuel Reed, a
Marblehead fisherman. "Mammy Red," as the
Marbleheaders used to call her, had long been
counted a witch, but her performances never
troubled her neighbors in the least. They did
not think of complaining of her. It remained
for the girls of Salem Village to do that. This
woman, so runs the tradition, used to wish that
"bloody cleavers" might be found on the cradles
of certain children, and whenever the wish was

uttered, of course, the cleaver was found there and the child sickened and died. She would "cause milk to curdle as soon as it left the cow." "Newly-churned butter turned to wool when it came in contact with Mammy Red."[5] The warrant for her arrest was issued May 28. The arrest was made on the 31st, and the examination held on the same day. She was charged with practicing witchcraft on Mary Walcott, Mercy Lewis and others. James Smith, constable of Marblehead, on May 31, returned that he had apprehended the said Reed and brought her to the house of Lieut. Ingersoll in Salem. She had little to say on examination, save that she knew nothing of the matter charged against her. Her trial before the court of Oyer and Terminer developed no new facts. Two indictments were presented, one for afflicting Elizabeth Booth on May 31 and divers other days, and the other for afflicting Elizabeth Hubbard on May 31 and divers other days. One thing is noticeable here as in many other of these indictments : that the indictment is not for afflicting any of the persons named in the original complaint, nor is the offence alleged the same as in the warrant of arrest. In most of the indictments the crime is alleged to have been committed on the day of the preliminary examination and in the court room. At the preliminary

5 Road's Hist. and Traditions of Marblehead, 31.

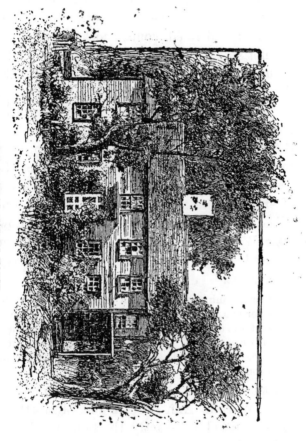

THE THOMAS HAINES HOUSE.
[Haines a witness against How.]

examination of Goodwife Reed, Abigail Williams had a fit. Mercy Lewis said Reed pinched her. Mary Walcott said she brought the book to her. Ann Putnam said Reed never hurt her, but she had seen her hurt others. Elizabeth Hubbard said Reed would knock her down if she did not sign. Ann Putnam cried out that she brought the book to her " just now." Elizabeth Booth fell into a fit, and Mary Walcott and Ann Putnam said Reed afflicted her. " Susan Sheldon," continues the report, " ordered to go to the examinant, was knocked down ; being carried to Reed in a fit was made well after Reed grasped her arm. Elizabeth Hubbard dealt with after the same manner." Reed " looked upon Elizabeth Hubbard and she was knocked down." Abigail Williams and John Indian being carried to Reed in a fit, were made well by her grasping their arms.

"This examinant being often urged what she thought these persons ailed would reply, I can not tell. Then being asked if she did not think they were bewitched, she answered, I can not tell. And being urged for her opinion in the case,—all she would say was, my opinion is they are in a sad condition."

At her trial on September 14, Mary Walcott, Mary Warren, Ann Putnam and Elizabeth Hubbard testified in exactly the same words, that, before the first examination, a woman came to each of them and said her name was Reed, and that on the day of examination they saw her afflict others. Charity Pitman and Sarah Dodd testified to a wordy encounter between Reed and a woman of the name of Syms, five years previously, in which Reed wished certain troubles might come to Syms, and soon after it " fell out with Mrs. Syms according to Reed's wish."

We have little information concerning Margaret Scott of Rowley. No doubt there were numerous papers in her case but they have been lost or destroyed. Only a few remain. Her preliminary examination took place on August 5, the arrest having probably been made on the previous day. I am unable to find anything about her or her family from the records or from the writings of local historians. Margaret Scott was tried at the September sitting of the court and sentenced on the 17th. She was executed on Thursday, the 22d. Francis Wyman testified during her trial, " that quickly after the first court at Salem about witchcraft, Margaret Scott or her appearance came to him and did most grievously torment him by choking and almost pressing him to death, and he believed in his heart that Margaret Scott was a witch." Phillip Nelson and his wife testified that for

" Two or three years before Robert Shilleto died we have often heard him complaining of Margaret Scott for hurting of him and often said that she was a witch, and so he continued complaining, saying he should never be well so long as Margaret Scott lived, and so he complained of Margaret Scott until he died."

Most of the evidence against this woman related to affairs that transpired five or ten years previous to 1692.

Sarah Wildes, wife of John Wildes of Salem Village and Topsfield, was arrested April 22, on a warrant issued the day before. John Buxton and Thomas Putnam went down to Salem from the Village on the 21st, and complained to the justices of Mrs. Wildes. The justices issued their warant to Marshal Herrick to arrest her and bring her to Lieut. Nathaniel Ingergoll's "to-morrow about ten of the clock." She was then examined, during which time Bibber and others claimed to see her on the beam of the meeting house. The usual circle of accusing girls was present and they "performed" after their customary manner. Sarah Wildes was committed to jail where she remained until June 29, when she was tried before the higher court, found guilty and sentenced to be hanged. On Tuesday, July 19, she went to that court above where no errors are made in the final judgment. The Wildes family belonged to the faction in Topsfield which was active in the feud with Salem Village. It is not possible to say whether this in any way influenced the prosecutors of Sarah Wildes. Ephriam Wildes, son of Sarah, deposed that the marshal of Salem came to Topsfield with the warrants for the arrest of his mother and William Hobbs and his wife. The

marshal served that on Sarah Wildes, and young
Wildes arrested Hobbs and wife. Subsequently
they accused his mother, and he thought it
might be because he arrested them.

As we have already seen, Martha Carrier and
Mary Parker were of Andover. So, too, was
Samuel Wardwell. Andover was particularly
unfortunate during the rage of the witchcraft
delusion. It suffered more than any place save

WIDOW MARY PUTNAM HOUSE.
[Mother of John Putnam, grandmother of Gen. Israel Putnam.
Gen. Putnam born here.]

Salem Village. The outbreak there, although
closely connected with that in the Village, was
yet somewhat independent of it. The wife of
Joseph Ballard of the town had been ill some
time, and the local physician could not help her.
In the spring of 1692 Ballard, hearing of the
" cases of torment " at the Village, sent down
there to have Ann Putnam come up and see if

she could discover any witchcraft about his wife's case. She came, accompanied by one of her companions. They were received with much pomp and solemnity, almost with superstition befitting a tribe of barbarians. The people gathered in the meeting-house, where the Rev. Mr. Barnard offered prayer. The girls then proceeded to the home of Mrs. Ballard and at once named certain persons who, they alleged, were tormenting her. These persons were forthwith arrested and sent to jail. Before the excitement ceased, nearly fifty persons had been arrested. Among them were Mary Osgood, wife of a deacon of the church; Abigail Faulkner and Elizabeth Johnson, daughters of Rev. Francis Dane, the senior pastor of the church; two of Mrs. Faulkner's daughters and one of Mrs. Johnson's; Mrs. Deliverance Dane, daughter-in-law of the minister; Samuel Wardwell and Ann Foster, besides Carrier and Mary Parker. Intimations were made that Mr. Dane himself and Justice Dudley Bradstreet, Mrs. Bradstreet, his wife, and his brother John, were not free from suspicion. John was charged with bewitching a dog,[6] and the animal was executed, as was another in the same town said to be bewitched. The Bradstreets fled the colony. Ann Foster died in prison. Abigail Faulkner was tried, convicted and sentenced, but subsequently re-

6 Mass. Hist. Coll., V., 71.

prieved.[7]   Samuel Wardwell was found guilty
and executed.   Sarah, his wife, Elizabeth Johnson and Mary Lacey were tried the following
January and convicted.   They were sentenced
to be hanged, but the proclamation of Gov. Phips
set them free.   The papers in the case of Samuel Wardwell are quite numerous and are interesting.   Wardwell was about forty-six years of
age, and appears to have been a good average
citizen of the times.   He was taken before the
local magistrates for examination on September
1.   What he said then we know not, but from
his subsequent testimony it is evident that he
denied the charge of witchcraft in the most
positive terms.   He was sent to jail to await
the action of the grand jury.   That body returned two indictments : or at least that is all
that are now on file.   One charged that
Samuel Wardwell practiced witchcraft on Martha Sprague of Boxford on August 15; the
other, that he, " about twenty years ago, with
the evill spiritt, the devill, a covenant did make
wherein he promised to honor, worship and
believe the devill, contrary to the statute of
King James the First, etc."   On the 13th of

7 Calef says because she was pregnant. (Fowler's Ed., 260.)
Upham says she made a partial confession, and that Sir William
ordered a reprieve, and after she had been thirteen weeks in
prison, he directed her to be discharged on the ground of insuf-
ficient evidence. He adds that this is the only instance of a
special pardon granted during the proceedings. (Salem Witchcraft, II., 332.)

September, Wardwell made a confession substantially as follows :

After returning several negative answers, he said he was
conscious he was in the snare of the devil. He had been
much discontented that he could get no more work done :
and that he had been foolishly led along with telling of for-
tunes which some times came to pass. He used also when
any creature came into his field to bid the devil take it, and
it may be the devil took advantage of him by that.

Constable Foster of Andover said this Wardwell told him once in the woods that when he
was a young man he could make all his cattle
come round about him when he pleased. The
said Wardwell, being urged to tell the truth, he
proceeded thus :

" That being once in a discontented frame he saw some
cats with the appearance of a man who called himself the
prince of the air, and promised him he should live comfort-
ably and be captain, and required said Wardwell to honor
him which he promised to do, and it was about twenty
years ago. He said the reason of his discontent then
was because he was in love with a maid named Barker who
slighted his love." He added that he covenanted with the
devil until he should be sixty years and he was now about
forty.

Wardwell's wife and daughter appeared to
testify against him, probably to save their own
necks, which they succeeded in doing. He, however, repented of the false confession he had
made and retracted. The retraction cost him
his life. At some subsequent time the daughter
retracted her confession against her father and
mother. Probably it was after Wardwell had

been hung. This case of Wardwell's is the only instance, so far as we know, where a husband and wife accused each other. Cases of children accusing parents and parents accusing children were, as we have seen, quite common. Wardwell was hanged with that group of eight which suffered on Thursday, September 22. When he stood on the gallows and was speaking to the people, a puff of tobacco smoke blew in his face and caused him to cough, whereupon the accusers said the devil hindered him with smoke.[8]

8 Calef, Fowler's Ed., 262.

CHAPTER XI.

ACCUSED AND TRIED BUT NOT EXECUTED.

purpose in this chapter, briefly to sketch some of the more peculiar and interesting features connected with a few trials of persons accused of witchcraft in 1692, but not executed, and in several cases not convicted. The case of Mary Perkins Bradbury of Salisbury is one of them. Mrs. Bradbury was the wife of Thomas Bradbury, and was seventy-five years of age. Some of those living near her had spoken of her as a witch long previous to 1692. In July of that year she was examined and committed to jail. Her trial took place at the early September session of the court. Two indictments against her have come down to us. To these indictments Mary Bradbury answered; "I do plead not guilty. I am wholly innocent of any such wickedness." It is difficult to say just when Mrs. Bradbury's preliminary examination took place. I find testimony against her by George Herrick given on May 26. On July 28

her husband testified that they had lived together fifty-five years, and that his wife had eleven
children and four grand-children. Her trial
before the upper court occupied the whole or a
part of three days. Testimony was given on
September 7, 8, and 9. She was convicted and
sentenced, but for some reason was not executed.
I presume it was owing to her high character
and the powerful influences brought to bear to
secure pardon. From the depositions on file we
are enabled to gather something of interest regarding her life and the complications of her
family with that of Mrs. Ann Putnam. Mrs.
Putnam, wife of Thomas Putnam of Salem Village, was daughter of George Carr of Salisbury.
The Carr and Bradbury families came into conflict under somewhat peculiar circumstances,
and when Mrs. Bradbury was brought to trial
most of the Carr family appeared to testify
against her.

The story of the trouble between the families
is, briefly, this : James Carr and William Bradbury, the latter, son of Mary Bradbury, were
paying attention, or trying to, to the widow
Maverick, daughter of Mr. Wheelright. Carr
deposed in 1692, that about twenty years before,
he was invited most courteously by the widow to

" Come oftener, and within a few days after one evening
I went thither again, and when I came thither again, William Bradbury was there who was then a suitor to the said

widow, but I did not know it till afterwards. After I came in the widow did so coursely treat the said William Bradbury that he went away seeming very angry. Presently after this I was taken after a strange manner as if living creatures did run about every part of my body ready to tear me to pieces. And so I continued for about three quarters of a year, by times, and I applied myself to Dr. Crosby, who gave me a great deal of physic but could make none work. Though he steeped tobacco in bosset drink he could make none to work, whereupon he told me that he believed I was behaged. And I told him I had thought so a good while. And he asked me by whom, and I told him I did not care for speaking, for one was counted an honest woman, but he urging me I told him and he said he believe that Mrs. Bradbury was a great deal worse than Good Martin."

After this, one night, something like a cat came to Carr in bed. He went to strike it off but could not move hand or foot for a while. Finally he did hit it and since then physic had worked on him.

Richard Carr testified that,

" About thirteen years ago, presently after some difference had happened to be between my honored father, Mr. George Carr, and Mrs. Bradbury, the prisoner at the bar, upon a Sabbath at noon, as we were riding home, by the house of Capt. Thomas Bradbury, I saw Mrs. Bradbury go into her gate, turn the corner of, and immediately there darted out of her gate a blue boar, and darted at my father's horse's legs, which made him stumble, but I saw it no more. And my father said, ' boys, what do you see?' We l oth answered, ' a blue boar.' "

Young Zerubabel Endicott, who was present on this occasion testified to the same, and also that he " saw the blue boar dart from Mr. Carr's

horse's legs in at Mrs. Bradbury's window."
William Carr, son of George, and brother of Mrs.
Ann Putnam, gave testimony in favor of Mrs.
Bradbury. He testified that he was with his
brother when he died, and that he "died peace-
fully and quietly, never manifesting trouble
about anybody, nor did he say anything about
Mrs. Bradbury or any one else doing him hurt."
Here is a piece of testimony that illustrates the
condition of mind of the people in 1692. It
shows how everyday occurrences, as we should
now call them, were attributed to supernatural
agencies. We may not wonder that a rough
sailor should some times believe in other than
human agencies as the cause of unusual events,
but not only did the rough sailor believe in
them, but the judges and the highest officials in
the province believed in them enough to admit
the evidence to convict, and to pass sentence of
death on the strength of that evidence. The
testimony to which I refer is that of Samuel
Endicott, thirty-one years of age. He testified:

About eleven years ago, being bound upon a voyage to
sea with Capt. Samuel Smith, late of Boston, deceased,
just before we sailed Mrs. Bradbury of Salisbury, the prisoner now at the bar, came to Boston with some firkins of
butter, of which Capt. Smith bought two. One of them
proved half-way butter and after we had been at sea three
weeks our men were not able to eat it, it stunk so, and run
with maggots, which made the men very much disturbed
about it, and would often say that they heard Mrs. Bradbury was a witch, and that they verily believed she was so,

or else she would not have served the Capt. so as to sell him such butter. And further this deponent testifieth, that in four days after they set sail they met with such a storm that we lost our main mast and rigging and lost fifteen horses, and that about a fortnight after, we set our Jersey mast, and that very night there came up a ship by our side and carried away two of the mizzen shrouds and one of the leaches of the main sail. And this deponent further sayeth that after they arrived at Barbadoes and went to Saltitudos and had laden their vessel, the next morning she sprang a leak in the hold, which wasted several tons of salt insomuch that we were forced to unlade our vessel again wholly to stop our leak. There was then four foot of water in the hold. After we had taken in our lading again we had a good passage home, but when we came near the land the Capt. sent this deponent forward to look out for land in a bright moonshining night, and as he was sitting upon the windlass he heard a rumbling noise under him. With that he, the said deponent, testifieth that he looked on the side of the windlass and saw the legs of some person, being no ways frighted, and that presently he was shook and looked over his shoulder and saw the appearance of a woman from the middle upwards, having a white cap and white neck cloth on her which then affrighted him very much, and as he was turning of the windlass he saw the aforesaid two legs.

This deposition bears date September 9, 1692. The substance of the testimony used to convict an intelligent, high minded woman of a capital crime, is, that some butter that she sold to a sea captain, if she did sell it to him, became rancid after the vessel got into a hot climate, and that the vessel sprung aleak. On these grounds the sailors concluded she was a witch. After that it was easy to see her appearance or most anything else.

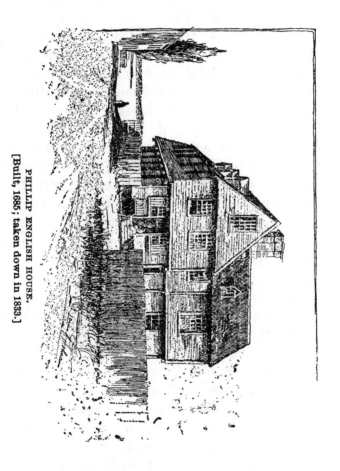

PHILIP ENGLISH HOUSE.
[Built, 1685; taken down in 1833.]

The story of the arrest and examination of Phillip English and his wife Mary, if we had all the documents in the case, would, no doubt, be exceedingly interesting. The papers have not come down to us save in the most meagre form. Phillip English was a wealthy merchant of Salem, and, in 1692, lived on Essex street, between what are now Webb and English streets. He occupied one of the finest mansions of the town, and perhaps of the colony. English owned fourteen buildings in Salem, a wharf and twenty-one vessels.[1] How charges of witchcraft came to be made against him and his wife has always been a mystery. Dr. Bently intimates that his controversies and law-suits with the town, and the superior style in which the family lived may have had something to do with leading the accusing children to name them. We are indebted to the same authority for our information about the arrest of Mrs. English. She was in bed when the sheriff came for her. The servants admitted him to her chamber, where he read the warrant. Guards were then placed around the house until morning, when she was taken away for examination. It is related that the pious mother attended to family devotions as usual that morning, kissed her children goodby, and calmly discussed their future in case she never returned to them. She then told the of-

1 Essex Inst. Hist. Coll., I., 161.

ficer she was ready to die.[2] Mrs. English was examined on April 22, and committed to jail. The warrant against her husband was issued on April 30. It was returned May 2, with the endorsement by the sheriff, "Mr. Phillip English not to be found." His arrest was not effected until May 30. He was then examined and committed to jail along with his wife. They soon escaped from jail and went to New York, where they lived until the storm had passed. They then returned to Salem and resumed their customary life.

The record of the prosecution of the Hobbs family constitutes an interesting chapter of witchcraft history. Abigail, the daughter, was the first to be arrested. The warrant against her was issued on April 18. It is said she was a reckless, vagabond creature, wandering through the woods at night like a half deranged person. The arrest of her father, William Hobbs, and her mother, Deliverance Hobbs, was effected three days later, mainly on the strength of statements made by the daughter. She charged that both of them were witches. Hobbs was about fifty years of age and lived on Topsfield territory. Abigail was examined in Salem prison on April 20, and stated, among other things, that the devil came to her in the shape of a man and brought images of the girls for

2 Ibd.

her to stick pins into. She did stick thorns into them and they "cried out." On May 12, she was again examined in prison.

Did Mr. Burroughs bring you any of the puppits of his wives to stick pins into?—I do not remember that he did.

Have any vessels been cast away by you?–I do not know.

She testified that she stuck thorns into people whom she did not know, and one of them, Mary Lawrence, suggested to her mind by the court, died.

Who brought the images to you?—It was Mr. Burroughs.

How did he bring it to you?—In his own person, bodily.

This is one of the most remarkable statements made in the whole history of the delusion. At the time Abigail Hobbs made it she was in jail, and had been since before the arrest of Burroughs. Previous to her arrest he was in Maine, eighty miles distant. Yet, she declares that Burroughs came to her *in his bodily person*, bringing images of a half dozen girls for her to afflict by sticking thorns into them, and that when she pricked them thus the real girls cried out from pain and she heard them. That there might be no mistake about this, seemingly, the magistrate asked, speaking of another party, whom she said she had thus afflicted, "Was he (Burroughs) there himself with you *in bodily person*?" Her answer was: "Yes, and so he was when he appeared to tempt me to set my hand to the book; he then appeared *in person*

and I *felt his hand* at the same time." This last
statement is stronger than the first; it leaves no
question as to what was meant by " bodily person." Before concluding her testimony she declared that she had " killed " " both boys and
girls." Abigail was examined before the magistrates on June 29. At her trial in September,
the following testimony was given :—

lidia Nichols aged about 7 years testifieth and saith that
about a yeare and a halfe agoe I asked abigaill hobs how
she dars¹ lie out a nights in ye woods alon she told me she
was not a fraid of anything for she told me she had sold
herself body and soule to ye old boy. and sins this about a
fortnight agoe ye said abigaill hobs & her mother came to
our hous my father & mother being not at home she began
to be rude & to behave herself unseemly I told her I wonder
she was not ashamed she bide me hold my tong or elce she
would rays all the folks thereabouts & bid me look there was
old crat en sate over the bedstead then her mother told her
shee lit le thought to abin the mother of such a dafter.
Elizabeth Nichols aged about 12 years testifieth ye same
she said at our house about a fortnight agoe

When William Hobbs and his wife came before the magistrates they were confronted with
the confession of their daughter, in which she
had charged them with being witches. They
were astounded. Mrs. Hobbs said she regretted
that she ever brought into the world such a
child. She indignantly denied being a witch, at
first. Finally, after long questioning, a confession was secured from her, in which she charged
her husband and young child with witchcraft.
The paper containing the record of the examina-

JOHN PUTNAM, 3RD, HOUSE, DANVERS.

tion of William Hobbs has suffered mutilation by reason of much handling and neglect in years past. Enough remains, however, to show that he stood immovable amid the storm of superstition that beat around him. He protested his innocence to the end.

What say you, asked Hathorne, are you guilty?—I can speak in the presence of God supremely, he answered, as I must look to give account another day that I am as clear as a new born babe.

Clear of what?—Of witchcraft.

Have you never hurt these?—No.

He is going to Mercy Lewis, said Abigail Williams, and Lewis fell in a fit. He is coming to Mary Walcott, was Williams next cry, and Walcott had a fit.

" How can you be clear when your appearance is thus seen producing such effect before our eyes?" queried the court. He was reminded of his wife's confession but that failed to move him. The examination was continued some time, interspersed with halloos, shrieks and wild out-cries from the accusing girls. Then Hathorne asked, " Can you now deny it?"—" I can," was the answer, " deny it to my dying day." After further efforts to make him confess, and continued refusals, Hobbs was sent to jail. He remained there until the middle of December when John Nichols and Joseph Towne bailed him. He failed to appear at the January term and was defaulted, but at the May term he answered to the summons, and the default was

taken off. In the Governor's proclamation free-
ing all the accused, Hobbs was included and
went at liberty. Abigail Hobbs was convicted
in the higher court and sentenced to be hanged,
but the sentence was never executed. Deliverance Hobbs lay in jail a long time. She does
not appear ever to have been tried, and it is certain that she was not executed.

Dorcas Hoar of Beverly, a widow, was arrested
on a warrant issued April 30, and examined at
Lieut. Ingersoll's on May 2. Elizabeth Hubbard
complained that the prisoner pinched her, showing the marks to the standers-by. The marshal
said she pinched her fingers at the same time.
" Dorcas Hoar," demanded the magistrate,
" why do you hurt these?"—" I never hurt a
child in my life," was the response. Not satisfied with this the accusers told her she killed
her husband, and charged her with various other
crimes. They said they saw " the black man
whispering in her ear." These calumnies were
too much for her to endure in silence, and she
cried back to them indignantly, " Oh, you are
liars, and God will stop the mouths of liars."
" You are not to speak after this manner in the
court," chided Hathorne. " I will speak the
truth as long as I live, was the brave and de-
fiant reply. She was committed for trial, and
subsequently convicted and sentenced. Notwithstanding her courageous words, Dorcas

Hoar was brought to a confession. Judge Sewall, under date of Sept. 21, says :

" A petition is sent to town in behalf of Dorcas Hoar who now confesses. Accordingly an order is sent to the sheriff to forbear her execution notwithstanding her being in the warrant to die tomorrow. This is the first condemned person who has confessed."[3]

During the trial of Dorcas, Abigail Williams declared that she saw the appearance of this woman before ever she saw Tituba Indian or any one else. This, if true, would make Dorcas Hoar the first of the witches of 1692. She escaped from jail in the same mysterious manner that so many other of the accused did. These escapes were numerous during the witchcraft trials. Whether the jails were weakly constructed, or the jailers did not guard the prisoners closely at all times, it is not possible to say. It is possible that high officials some times connived at the escape of accused persons. Most of these escapes were from the Boston jail, which would naturally be as strong as any.[4] On the other hand, the Ipswich jail was a very primitive structure and escape from it must have been easy, yet no one, accused of witchcraft, ever escaped from it.

The case of Nehemiah Abbott is of interest,

3 Sewall Papers, I., 365.
4 Phillip English and wife were allowed the freedom of the town under bonds, being required only to sleep in jail. Essex Inst. Hist. Col., I., 161.

because, so far as known, he is the only person who was released after refusing to confess. Abbott was arrested at the same time as William Hobbs, April 21. He was examined on the following day. At first all the accusing girls said he had afflicted them, and fell into fits. Ann Putnam "saw him on the beam." Others identified him as one who had appeared to them Asked to confess and find mercy, he replied, "I speak before God that I am clear in all respects." The girls "were all struck dumb" again. Suddenly Mercy Lewis said: "It is not the man." Other accusers wavered. Ann Putnam said that the reason she had declared Abbott to be the man was because the devil put a mist before her eyes. The case completely broke down and Abbott was released. One question suggests itself very forcibly in this connection: If Abbott was not the man who afflicted these girls at the time, why did they fall down when he had looked on them? and why did they have fits in the court room? Parris in his account of the trial says, when Abbott was

"Brought in again, by reason of much people, and many in the windows, so that the accusers could not have a clear view of him, he was ordered to be abroad and the accusers to go forth to him and view him in the light, which they did in the presence of the magistrates and many others, discoursed quietly with him, one and all acquitting him, but yet said he was like the man, but he had not the wen they saw in his apparition. Note, he was a hilly faced man, and stood shaded by reason of his own hair, so that for a time he seemed to some bystanders and observers to be considerably like the person the afflicted did describe."

Mary Warren was, as I have mentioned in preceding pages, one of the early and persistent accusers. She was twenty years of age and a servant in the family of John Procter. She gave testimony against some of those first charged, but afterwards became skeptical and began to talk about the deceptions of the afflicted, and said they "did but dissemble." The other accusing girls then cried out against her, and she spoke still more emphatically against the prosecutions. A warrant for her arrest was procured on April 18, and she was examined the following day. Parris kept the official record of that examination. He says, when she was coming towards the bar, the afflicted fell into fits. The magistrates told her she was charged with witchcraft and asked: "Are you guilty or not?" To this she replied: "I am innocent." When the afflicted were asked if she had hurt them, some were dumb, and Hubbard "testified against her." All the afflicted soon had fits. Then Mary Warren fell into a fit, and some cried out that she was going to confess, "but," continues the report, "Goody Corey and Procter and his wife came in in their apparitions, and struck her down, and said she should tell nothing." Then followed one of the most dramatic scenes in the whole witchcraft history.

The official record of the examination says :—[5]

After continuing in a fit some time she said, I will speak, Oh, I am sorry for it, I am sorry for it. Wringing her hands she fell into another fit. Then attempting a little later to speak her teeth were set. She fell into another fit and shouted, O Lord help me. O good Lord, save me. And then afterwards cried again, I will tell, I will tell, and then fell into a dead fit again.

And afterwards cried I will tell, I will tell, they did, they did, they did, and then fell into a violent fit again.

After a little recovery, she cried, I will tell, I will tell. They brought me to it. And then fell into a fit again, which fits continuing, she was ordered to be led out, and the next to be brought in, viz., Bridget Bishop.

She was called in again, but immediately taken with fits. Have you signed the devil's book?—No.

Then she fell into fits again, and was sent forth for air. After a considerable space of time she was brought in again, but could not give account of things by reason of fits and so sent forth.

Mary Warren was called in afterwards in private before magistrates and ministers. She said I shall not speak a word, but I will, I will speak, Satan. She saith she will kill me. Oh, she saith she owes me a spite, and will claw me off. Avoid Satan, for the name of God, avoid. And then fell into fits again, and cried, Will ye? I will prevent ye in the name of God.

It will be understood that Mary Warren, all this time, was struggling to confess and the devil sought to prevent her. At least, that is what she was pretending. Whether it was a piece of the most perfect acting, we do not know. Yet we do know now that there was no reality about the witchcraft pretensions from be-

5 Essex Court Papers.

ginning to end. Mr. Parris notes that not one of
the sufferers was afflicted during her examination after she began to confess. Is it possible
that the whole performance with Mary Warren
was a part of a conspiracy between her and
the other accusing girls and the older prosecutors? It is possible, but hardly probable. She
made a second and circumstantial confession, in
which she turned state's evidence, so to speak,
and told all she had seen and heard. She was
immediately released and returned to her former occupation of testifying against persons accused of witchcraft. The impression which her
case made on the credulous people of Salem was
to convince them that there was no fraud about
the witchcraft accusations and prosecutions
when members of the accusing circle were " cried
out against " by one of their companions, and
that if she could tear herself from the devil's
snare, the others could do the same if so disposed.

Jonathan Carey, whose wife was charged with
witchcraft, has left a circumstantial account of
his wife's examination before the magistrates.
It gives a clear idea of the mode of procedure,
which did not differ in this case from that followed in others. Capt. Carey was an old ship-
master, and a man whose word was not to be
doubted. He says :—

May 24. I having heard some days, that my wife was

accused of witchcraft; being much disturbed at it, by advice went to Salem Village, to see if the afflicted knew her·
We arrived there on the 24th of May. It happened to be a
day appointed for examination, accordingly, soon after our
arrival, Mr. Hathorne and Mr. Corwin, &c., went to the
meeting-house, which was the place appointed for that
work. The minister began with prayer; and, having taken
care to get a convenient place, I observed that the afflicted
were two girls of about ten years old, and about two or
three others of about eighteen. One of the girls talked
most, and could discern more than the rest. The prisoners
were called in one by one, and, as they came in, were
cried out at, &c. The prisoners were placed about seven or
eight feet from the justices and the accusers were between
the justices and them. The prisoners were ordered to
stand right before the justices, with an officer appointed to
hold each hand, lest they should therewith afflict them.
And the prisoner's eyes must be constantly on the justices,
for, if they looked on the afflicted, they would either fall
into fits, or cry out of being hurt by them. After an examination of the prisoners, who it was afflicted these girls, and
c., they were put upon saying the Lord's prayer, as a trial
of their guilt. After the afflicted seemed to be out of their
fits, they would look steadfastly on some one person, and
frequently not speak, and then the justices said they were
struck dumb, and after a little time would speak again.
Then the justices said to the accusers, " Which of you will
go and touch the prisoner at the bar?" Then the most
courageous would adventure, but, before they had made
three steps, would ordinarily fall down as in a fit. The
justices ordered that they should be taken up and carried
to the prisoner, that she might touch them, and as soon as
they were touched by the accused, the justices would say:
" They are well," before I could discern any alteration,—by
which I observed that the justices understood the manner
of it. Thus far I was only as a spectator. My wife also
was there part of the time, but no notice was taken of her
by the afflicted, except once or twice they came to her and
asked her name.

But I, having an opportunity to discourse Mr. Hale with whom I had formerly acquaintance, I took his advice what I had best do, and desired of him that I have an opportunity to speak with her that accused my wife; which he promised should be, I acquainting him that I reposed my trust in him. Accordingly he came to me after the examination was over, and told me I had now an opportunity to speak with the said accuser, Abigail Williams, a girl eleven or twelve years old, but that we could not be in private at Mr. Parris's house, as he had promised me; we went therefore into the ale-house, where an Indian man attended us, who, it seems, was one of the afflicted; to him we gave some cider; he showed several scars, that seemed as if they had been long there, and showed them as done by witchcraft, and acquainted us that his wife, who also was a slave, was in prison for witchcraft. And now, instead of one accuser, they all came in, and began to tumble down like swine; and then all three women were called in to attend them. We in the room were all at a stand to see who they would cry out of; but in a short time they cried out, "Carey;" and immediately after, a warrant was sent from the justices to bring my wife before them, who was sitting in a chamber near by, waiting for this. Being brought before the justices, her chief accusers were two girls. My wife declared to the justices, that she never had any knowledge of them before that day. She was forced to stand with her arms stretched out. I requested that I might hold one of her hands, but it was denied me. Then she desired me to wipe the tears from her eyes, and the sweat from her face, which I did; then she desired she might lean herself on me, saying she should faint. Justice Hathorne replied she had strength enough to torment these persons, and she should have strength to stand. I speaking something against their cruel proceedings, they commanded me to be silent, or else I should be turned out of the room. The Indian before mentioned was also brought in, to be one of her accusers, being come in, he now (when before the justices) fell down, and tumbled about like a hog, but said nothing. The justices asked the girls who afflicted the Indian: they answered, she (meaning my wife), and that she now lay upon him. The justices ordered her to touch him, in order to his cure, but her head must be turned another way, lest, instead of curing, she should make him worse by her looking at him, her hand being guided to take hold of his, but the Indian took hold of her hand and pulled her down on the floor in a barberous manner; then his hand was taken off, and her hand put on his, and the cure was quickly wrought.

Capt. Carey said he had difficulty to get a bed for his wife that night. She was committed to jail in Boston, and subsequently removed to Cambridge. "Having been there one night, next night the jailer put irons on her legs ; the weight was about eight pounds." These irons and other afflictions threw her into convulsions, and he tried to have the irons taken off, but in vain. When the trials came on Carey went to Salem to see how they were conducted. Finding that spectral testimony and idle gossip were admitted as evidence, he told his wife she had nothing to hope for there. He procured her escape from jail and they went to New York, where Gov. Fletcher befriended them.

John Alden, sen., of Boston, also wrote an account of how accused people were treated. Alden was son of the famous John Alden, one of the founders of the Plymouth colony. He had resided in Boston thirty years, was a member of the church there, and had commanded an armed vessel belonging to the colony. He was seventy years of age and quite wealthy. Alden

WITCH PINS, SALEM COURT HOUSE.

was sent for on May 28, and went to Salem Village on the 31st. Gedney, Hathorne and Corwin sat at his examination. It differed but little from that described by Capt. Carey. It was some time before the accusing girls learned who Alden was, and in the mean time they pointed to others as their tormentors. Finally they saw Alden and cried out against him. They were all ordered to go down into the street, says Alden, where a ring was made and the same accuser cried out, "there stands Alden, a bold fellow, with his hat on before the judges, he sells powder and shot to the Indians and French, and lies with the Indian squaws, and has Indian papooses." "Then was Alden committed to the marshal's custody, and his sword taken from him." The magistrates "bid Alden look upon the accusers, which he did and they fell down. Alden asked Mr. Gedney what reason there could be given why Alden's looking on *him* did not strike *him* down as well, but no reason was given." Alden was sent to jail, but he too saw no hope if brought to trial before the court as constituted, and made his escape.

Rebecca Eames, wife of Robert Eames, on the day Mr. Burroughs and his companion martyrs were hung, was a spectator of the scene at a house near Gallows hill. While in this house the woman whose guest she was felt a pin stuck in her foot. She immediately accused Rebecca

Eames of bewitching her, she " not being as good as she might have been." Goodwife Eames was immediately arrested, and was examined before the magistrates in Salem on August 19. Confessing herself a witch,

" She owned she had bin in ye snare a month or 2 & had bin perswaded to it: 3 months: & that ye devil apeared to her like a Colt very ugly: ye first time: but she would not own yt she had bin baptized by him she did not known but yt ye devil did persuade her to renounce god & christ & follow his wicked ways:"

She was committed to jail, tried the following month, convicted, and on the 17th, sentenced to be hanged. The sentence was never executed, but she remained in jail until the following March when she was reprieved. Her husband died on July 22, 1693, and she in 1721 at the age of 82.[6]

Sarah Buckley and Mary Whittredge, her daughter, were brought before the examining magistrates May 18, on warrants issued May 14. The accusing girls testified against Mrs. Buckley substantially as they had at the trials of other accused persons. Susan Sheldon declared that she " saw the black man whispering in her ear." She was committed to prison, where she remained until January, 1693, being heavily ironed all the time. William Hubbard " the venerable

6 The records of the Court of General Sessions of Jan. 18, 1692, show that Zerubabel Endicott was arraigned on charge of adultery with Rebecca Eames and bound over in the sum of £200.

minister of Ipswich," on June 20, 1692, certi-
fied to her high character. He had

> " Known her for above fifty years, and during all that
> time, I never knew nor heard of any evil in her carriage, or
> conversation unbecoming a Christian: likewise she was bred
> up by Christian parents all the time she lived here in Ips-
> wich." He was " strangely surprised that any person
> should speak or think of her as one worthy to be suspected
> of any such crime."

Rev. John Higginson, who had been a minister of the gospel for fifty-five years and pastor
of the First Church in Salem for a third of a
century, and Rev. Samuel Cheever, bore equally
strong testimony to the high character of Sarah
Buckley. The woman was probably ironed during her confinement in jail because of statements
of Mary Walcott. Benjamin Hutchinson, on
July 15, deposed that his wife being taken with
great pain he went for Mary Walcott " to come
and look to see if she could see any body upon
her ; and as soon as she came into the house she
said Sarah Buckley and Mary Whitridge were
upon his wife." These women, be it remembered, were already in jail. Hutchinson sent to
the sheriff, desiring him "to take some course
with those women that they might not have
such power to torment." The sheriff ordered
them to be fettered, and " ever since that "
Hutchinson's wife had been " tolerably well."
Sarah Buckley and Mary Whitridge were tried
in January, 1693, and acquitted. They were

poor people, and the costs of court, the expense of living in jail and the jailer's fee of £10, fairly impoverished them. It is difficult for us to realize the state of a community where persons accused of a terrible crime, kept heavily ironed for many months in a vile prison, tried for their lives, and finally acquitted, were compelled to pay all the costs and fees before being liberated.

There were many other persons tried or accused, and still others suspected, besides those individually mentioned in the preceding pages, but the particulars already given will suffice to indicate how all were treated. The course pursued by magistrates and courts differed only in minor details.

CHAPTER XII.

A REVIEW.

N reviewing the story presented in the preceding pages I confess to a measure of doubt as to the moving causes in this terrible tragedy. It seems impossible to believe a tithe of the statements which were made at the trials. And yet it is equally difficult to say that nine out of every ten of the men, women and children who testified upon their oaths, intentionally and wilfully falsified. Nor does it seem possible that they did, or could, invent all these marvelous tales ; fictions rivalling the imaginative genius of Haggard or Jules Verne. Nevertheless, we know that the greater portion of their depositions were without foundation in fact. Many of them we may attribute to the wild fancyings of minds disordered by the excited state of the community. Others cannot be thus explained satisfactorily. In order to form a correct judgment of the acts and words of these people, we must first put ourselves in the place of the men and women of 1692. They believed in witchcraft ; that there was such a thing, no one doubted. As we have seen, the wisest jurists, as well as all the ministers, believed in the existence of witches. Books were written upon the subject, as upon insanity and kindred topics. People had been arrested and executed for the alleged crime in all Christian countries. For nearly half a century previous to 1692, prosecutions were made for witchcraft in New England. Men like Gov. Endicott, Gov. Winthrop, and even the liberal-minded Bradstreet, had passed sentence upon its unfortunate victims. Shall we, then, wonder that the people of Salem Village attributed to the demon witchcraft the strange performances of Abigail Williams, Elizabeth Parris, Ann Putnam and their associates, in 1692 and 1693? Rather shall we not record our admiration that then and there the belief in spectral evidence, and, necessarily witchcraft, received its death blow. The refusal of the Essex jury to convict in January, 1693, was the beginning of the end, not only in Salem but in the world. Some characters were exhibited during the dark period that command our profoundest respect. Heroic Joseph Putnam always denounced the course being pursued and kept his horse saddled for some weeks in anticipation of a call from the constable and with the full determination to escape.

That Mr. Parris was sincere in the belief that these children were bewitched, I see no reason to doubt. That he " fanned the flame " and encouraged the prosecutions for the purpose of " wreaking vengeance " on his opponents in church affairs, as is often asserted, is doubtful. That he should be more ready to believe one of his opponents guilty than one of his friends and

JOSEPH PUTNAM HOUSE, DANVERS.

supporters, is quite natural, although we may look in vain for any positive evidence of even this. Families that supported him did not always escape prosecution, while others, not of the ministerial faction, were numbered among the most active accusers. Every neighborhood disagreement that court record or tradition has handed down to us, has been enlarged upon and embellished by different writers to prove that persons were accused of witchcraft because of

some differences of opinion or some petty suit-
at-law.   And yet we frequently find these same
people uniting in a complaint for witchcraft, as
in the case of Sarah Good, where the complainants were Thomas Preston, son-in-law of Rebecca
Nurse, and Thomas and Edward Putnam.   That
Parris should take an active part in the affair
was natural, seeing he was the minister of the
parish.   Is it matter of wonder that he should
attend the trials and ask questions?   He was
probably as familiar with the facts as any one
who could be present.   He was frequently reporter of the evidence, appointed by the court
because he wrote in characters and could make
minutes faster than most others.   It is true that
after the storm had past Parris had renewed disagreements with the church.   But it was really
a continuation of the old feud that had merely
slumbered for a year, together with the added
feelings engendered by the occurrences of that
period.   Naturally the activity of Mr. Parris in
the prosecutions rendered him obnoxious to the
surviving relatives of those whose lives were
taken.   All this, however, would be consistent
with his sincerity.   No one now questions but
that the whole unfortunate affair, judged from
our stand-point, was an error of the gravest
nature.   But judged from the vantage ground of
1692, the first error was in the conviction of
persons on purely spectral evidence, for which

the judges, not Parris, were responsible. The second was made by the judges when they failed to penetrate the veil of improbability which shrouded the testimony of many witnesses, and to see that much of this testimony was either falsehood or delusion. The judges, as we have seen, followed very closely the precedents of the ablest English jurists. All those engaged in the prosecutions appear to have learned a lesson by their experience. Parris himself subsequently said that, "were the same troubles again he should not agree with his former apprehension."[1] Granting that he even took up the witchcraft cry too hastily in the beginning, where is the evidence that he did it to "wreak vengeance" on any who had opposed his ministry? I mean not to defend Parris. Undoubtedly he was hasty. More care, a cooler head, better judgment, might have prevented the witchcraft tragedy. The delusion would have been ended almost before it was begun had the tricks of those girls been exposed. Parris could have done this had he not been blinded by the infatuation of his belief in witchcraft. But that he was actuated by motives of spite would appear to be very doubtful.

Even more has Cotton Mather's position been misunderstood and misinterpreted. He and his

[1] Samuel Parris' "Acknowledgement," 1694; quoted by Calef, Fowler's ed., 150.

father, Increase Mather, were conservative in all matters relating to the witchcraft prosecutions after they began. Cotton Mather has been charged repeatedly with " getting up " the delusion at Salem Village, with being " the chief agent of the mischief," and helping it on throughout that dark summer. On the contrary, he was not present at a single trial, and was at only one execution. It is an open question whether he was not at the execution of Mr. Burroughs as a friend and brother minister and not as a persecutor. We should take with some measure of allowance Calef's statement about Mather's declaration that Burroughs was no ordained minister. Mr. Mather advised the judges and the council to exercise great care, and not to convict on spectral evidence alone. It has been said that he advised testing the accused by having them repeat the Lord's prayer. So he did. But in doing so he especially enjoined the judges not to use it as evidence to convict. Here are his exact words :

" That they be tested by repeating the Lord's prayer or those other Sistems of christianity which it seems the divels often make the witches unable to repeat without ridiculous Depravations and Amputations. The danger of this experiment will be taken away if you make no evidence of it, but only put it to the use I mention. . . . The like I would say of some other experiments only we may venture too far before we are aware."[2]

2 Mass. Hist. Coll., VIII., 391.

At the very outset of the examination, Cotton Mather wrote to Maj. Richards,

"Most humbly begging him that he do not lay more stress on pure spectre testimony than it will bear. It is certain that the divils have sometimes represented the shapes of persons not only innocent but very vertuous."[3]

He wrote to Judge Sewall on Aug. 17, 1692:

" I do still Think That when there is no further Evidence against a person but only This, That a Spectre in their shape does afflict a neighbor, that Evidence is not enough to convict ye . . of witchcraft."

This letter was written two days before the execution of Proctor, Burroughs, Willard, Carrier and Jacobs, and therefore this further sentence is peculiarly significant:

" If any persons have been condemned about whom any of ye judges are not easy in their minds, that ye Evidence against them, has been satisfactory, it would certainly be for ye glory of the whole Transaction to give that person a Reprieve."[4]

That Cotton Mather believed in witchcraft, is not the question. We know he did in the strongest manner, and that he had written extensively in support of the doctrine. Nor is there any question but that he believed in the admission of spectral evidence. But the question is, how far would he go in the prosecutions and how much credence would he give to this evidence. It seems plain from quotations already

3 Ibd.
4 Transactions of the Lit. and Hist. Society of Quebec, II., 313.

made from his writings that, while he believed in the admission of the testimony he did not believe in convicting persons on it alone.   Phips wrote, on Feb. 21, 1693, that the advice given by the Mathers and other ministers for more caution in the admission of evidence, had much lessened the peril of conviction.[5]   Nevertheless, Cotton Mather was in a large degree responsible for the witchcraft troubles of 1692, because he had been for several years instilling into the minds of the people belief, not only in the reality of witch-craft, but in the existence of an ever present devil who was using the spectres of human beings to do his evil deeds.   Mather appears to have had an unbounded faith in his own knowl-edge and power ; he believed himself divinely appointed, above all his brother ministers, to lead in the work of purifying the community if not the world, and driving out the evil one.

Mr. Mather's plan for dealing with people supposed to be bewitched was to pray with them, not to prosecute the persons whom they accused of being their tormentors.   He seems to have been as successful with his remedy as the judges were with theirs.   He prayed with the Goodwin children and with their alleged tormentors.   That outbreak was checked in the family where it ori-ginated, and no lives were then sacrificed, beyond that of Mrs. Glover.   Perhaps if Mather had

5 Felt's Annals of Salem, II., 482.

been as active in the Salem Village witchcrafts
as some of his detractors allege, he would have
been the means of saving the lives that were
sacrificed to the law and the ill-timed activity
of Parris, Noyes, Hale, and the court. Brattle,
speaking of the execution of Burroughs and
others, at which Cotton Mather was present,
says :

" They protested their innocency as in the presence of the
great God whom forthwith they were to appear before;
they wished, and declared their wish , that their blood
might be the last innocent blood shed upon that account.
With great affectation they entreated Mr. C. M. to pray
with them; they prayed that God would discover what
witchcrafts were among us ; they forgave their accusers,
they spake without reflection on jury and judges for bringing them in guilty and condemning them : they prayed earnestly for pardon for all other sins and for an interest in
the precious blood of our dear Redeemer : and seemed to be
very sincere, upright, and sensible of their circumstances
on all accounts; especially Proctor and Willard, whose
whole management of themselves, from the Jail to the
Gallows, and whilst at the Gallows, was very affecting and
melting to the hearts of some considerable spectators, whom
I could mention to you: but they are executed and so I
leave them."[6]

The reader will have noticed, no doubt, that
the charges of witchcraft in 1692 were made
mainly by children, as in all previous cases in
this and other countries. Children were the accusers in nearly every instance ; children were
the afflicted, and children were the principal

6 Mass. Hist. Coll. (1st. series), V., 68.

witnesses. Little Ann Putnam testified in nineteen cases, Elizabeth Hubbard in twenty, Mary
Walcott in sixteen, Mary Warren in twelve,
Mercy Lewis in ten, Abigail Williams, Susan
Sheldon and Elizabeth Booth in eight each. In
fact, the delusion originated with children and
was kept alive by them. Shorn of their testimony, it could not have been maintained for a
day. Ann Putnam's power over life and death
exceeded that of judges and jury. When she
said Martha Corey was a witch, Martha was
arrested. When she said the man Abbott was
the one whose appearance had tormented her,
he was arrested. When she said he was not the
man, he was instantly released. What motives
prompted these children it is difficult to say. It
may be they were carried away by the importance in the community which their statements
gave them; or they may have been the victims
of the same mental derangement that afflicted
the older people. We do not know, we can
never know, what prompted them to act as they
did. The Carr family from which Ann Putnam
was descended, is known to have been one whose
members were very impressionable, given to fits
of nervousness and hysteria.

But how shall we account for the stories told
by the numerous adult witnesses? What explanation shall be offered for the marvelous
tales of Mrs. Ann Putnam, of Richard Carr,

Samuel Sheldon, Jonathan Westgate, Samuel Shattuck and others? Some statements by these witnesses are undoubtedly merely exaggerated accounts of every day occurrences. Others are not thus explainable. The only solution which we should be likely to offer of such tales in this day and generation, would be that the person's mind was badly disordered by insanity, or by habitual intemperance, or that he had suffered an attack of nightmare. It is pretty evident that the two disorders last named did effect the testimonies of some of the witnesses, but the solution that seems most reasonable is that which attributes the conduct of these persons to a sort of epidemic, which pervaded the whole community. Men and women were temporarily insane over the strange occurrences in their midst. Their minds were actually diseased. Many who confessed themselves witches subsequently explained that they did this "because so many people were positive the devil had appeared in their shapes, they could not doubt it was true." They had been educated to believe such things not only possible but probable and common. They did not know but that the demon had invisibly taken their shapes to torment others. Persons whom they did not suspect of intentionally falsifying, testified under oath that these things had been done, and they could not doubt it. The safest way therefore, as they well knew, was to confess. Others, no doubt did not believe the testimony against themselves, but acknowledged themselves to be witches because those who confessed were discharged, while those who did not were eventually convicted and executed. Some stood to the confession and were saved. Others, under the promptings of their consciences, repudiated the confession and suffered death. It is difficult to reconcile the conduct of Thomas Putnam, and his wife Ann, and their daughter Ann, jr., with other than motives of personal malice. Young Ann, as we have seen, was a leading complainant and witness in all the important cases. The mother testified at several trials, telling some of the most improbable stories recorded in all this history. Thomas was an active and leading character throughout from first to last. He prepared many of the depositions for his daughter, and on several occasions, made statements for her over his own signature. Why he was thus prominent does not clearly appear. It may be that he was prompted solely by what he believed to be for the public good : that he was honest, but misguided, yet his zeal was certainly extraordinary.

Of the conduct of the examining magistrates, the judges and other officials, but one opinion seems possible : they were misguided in their sense of duty, unjust to the accused, and unnec-

essarily severe with the prisoners. This is true
whether we judge them from the standpoint of
1892 or 1692. The accused were treated, from
the moment some babbling child uttered a suspic-
ious word against them, to the burial of their
bodies after execution, with a harshness sometimes little short of brutality, and with far
more severity than any evidence would indicate
that persons accused of other crimes in those
days were treated. They appear to have been
regarded as veritable devils themselves, ready to
torment everybody. Their rights, even as the
rights of accused persons were understood in
1692, were not protected. The treatment of
persons accused of witchcraft in England a half
century earlier, by courts and officers, was apparently more civilized and humane, so far as
any one can judge from the accounts left to us
of those trials. The great mistake of the judges
in Massachusetts was in allowing convictions on
spectral evidence alone, and in holding that the
devil could not appear in the shape of a person
without that person's consent, although they had
English precedents for this course. Stoughton
maintained this view throughout the entire
period, against the advice of some of his associates on the bench. It is not to be presumed
that he or any one else connected with these
prosecutions desired to convict innocent persons,
or to take the lives of any not proven guilty by

what seemed to them legitimate evidence. They undoubtedly believed that the word of a witch was not to be taken under any circumstances; that when the accused made any statements in their own behalf they were prompted to it by the devil, and therefore not to be believed.

One thing at least seems certain regarding the witchcraft prosecutions: nearly every man prominently connected with them subsequently confessed his error. Even Stoughton, in 1696, approved a proclamation ordaining a public fast to be kept on the 14th of January, 1697, to implore that the anger of God might be turned away, and concluding with the expression of a fear that something might still be wanting to accompany their supplications, especially as related to the witchcraft tragedy. The General Court subsequently reimbursed to the heirs of the executed persons and to those who were imprisoned from time to time during 1692-3 more or less of the losses suffered by them, and reversed the attainders. I am aware that it is a disputed question whether all the necessary formalities to make the several acts of the General Court of full force and effect were ever fulfilled; but there is no question that the sentiment of the people's representatives was overwhelmingly in favor of doing thus much to right a great wrong.

Rev. John Hale of Beverly, one of the ablest

divines in New England, repented of the part he had taken in the affair, and wrote that,

" By following such traditions of our fathers, maxims of the common law, and precedents and principles, which now we may see weighed in the balance of the sanctuary, are found too light—such was the darkness of that day, the tortures and lamentations of the afflicted, and the power of former precedents, that we walked in the clouds and could not see our way."

The First Church in Salem, by vote recorded, that " we are through God's mercy to us, convinced that we were at that dark day, under the power of those errors which then prevailed in the land.'"[7]   On July 8, 1703, the ministers of Essex county addressed a memorial to the General Court, saying there was " great reason to fear that innocent persons then suffered, and that God may have a controversey with the land upon that account."[8]   The jurors who tried and convicted the accused, united in a public statement in which they said, among other things : " We justly fear that we were sadly deluded and mistaken."   It may interest the reader to know who the jurymen were.   Neal gives the following list of one jury : Thomas Fisk, foreman, William Fisk, John Batchelder, Thomas Fisk, jun., John Dane, Joseph Eveleth, Thomas Perly, sen.; John Peabody, Thomas Perkins, Samuel Sayer, Andrew Elliott and Henry Herrick,

7 Records First Church, Salem.
8 Witchcraft Papers, State House, Boston.

sen. Ann Putnam lived to realize the error of her conduct, and to repent of it most bitterly. In 1706, Rev. Joseph Green, then pastor of the Village church, read her confession to the church. It was as follows :

I desire to be humbled before God for that sad and humbling providence that befel my father's family in the year about 1692; that I, then being in my childhood, should by such a providence of God, be made an instrument for the accusing of several persons of a grievous crime, whereby their lives were taken away from them, whom now I have just grounds and good reason to believe they were innocent persons; and that it was a great delusion of Satan that deceived me in that sad time, whereby I justly fear I have been instrumental, with others, though ignorantly and unwittingly, to bring upon myself and this land the guilt of innocent blood; though what was said or done by me against any person I can truly and uprightly say before God and man, I did it not out of any anger, malice or ill-will to any person, for I had no such thing against one of them, but what I did was ignorantly, being deluded of satan. And particularly as I was a chief instrument of accusing of goodwife Nurse and her two sisters, I desire to lie in the dust, and to be humbled for it, in that I was a cause, with others, of so sad a calamity to them and their families; for which cause I desire to lie in the dust, and earnestly beg forgiveness of God, and from all those unto whom I have given just cause of sorrow and offence, whose relations were taken away or accused.

Many others connected with the prosecutions subsequently acknowledged their error. None of these people, as I understand it, denied witchcraft itself. The error they acknowledged was as to the method of procedure. They confessed that they had been too hasty in their judgments, and had accused and convicted innocent persons.

Great stress has been laid on the so-called "confession" of Judge Sewall in the old South Church, Boston, on Fast Day, 1697. The act was nothing out of the usual course for Sewall, or for many others in that day. They had a habit, whenever any great joy or sorrow came to them or their families, of "putting up a bill" to be read from the pulpit. Sewall's diary shows that he did this often. It was not usually a confession of any special sin, but a "petition," he calls it. The governor had appointed a day of fasting and prayer. On that day Sewall handed his petition to the minister, and, as was the custom, stood up in his pew while it was being read. The petition was as follows :

Samuel Sewall, sensible of the reiterated strokes of God upon himself and family, and being sensible that as to the guilt contracted on the opening of the late Commission of oyer and Terminer at Salem (to which the order for this day relates) he is upon many accounts, more concerned than any he knows of, Desires to take the Blame and shame of it, Asking pardon of men, And especially desiring prayers that God who has an Unlimited Authority, would pardon that sin and all other his sins, personal and Relative. And according to his infinite Benignity and Soverignty Not Visit the sin of him or any other, upon himself or any of his, nor upon the Land. But that He would powerfully defend him against all Temptation to Sin, For the Future, and vouchsafe him the efficatious, saving Conduct of his Word and Spirit."9

9 Sewall Papers, I, 445.

These examples of repentance and change of sentiments might be continued almost indefinitely, but enough has been given to show that the leading prosecutors and the officials generally, subsequently acknowledged their mistake. The conclusion, therefore, which seems most rational is that which attributes the unfortunate affair to a species of neighborhood insanity, a wholesale delusion. It was like a cyclone that sweeps over the land, or a conflagration that wipes out of existence whole sections of a city. We do not realize the awful drama which is being enacted around us. Only when the storm has passed and we awake to a thorough comprehension of the calamity, do we appreciate its force ; then, the hour of its raging seems like a dream. Such, I judge, was substantially the case with our ancestors two centuries ago. They did not realize, during the summer of 1692, the awfulness of the tragedy they were enacting. They believed that they were casting out devils, and that any measures, however severe, were justifiable. Their language after the storm was passed and a calm had settled over the land, implies as much,—and more;—that the full realization of what they had been doing, dawned on them only after all was over. The witchcraft tragedy must then have seemed to them like a horrid nightmare. We of the present generation shudder at the intolerant persecutions and superstitions of our ancestors. Let us do nothing in politics or religion that will cause our descendants to blush for us. It is well to revive the unwise or unjust acts of our ancestors sometimes, as we would place a beacon on some shoal or reef where a ship had been wrecked, to warn others of the danger.

APPENDIX A.

For more convenient reference a list of all persons accused of witchcraft in 1692, so far as known, is appended.

The following were executed: June 10, Bridget Bishop; July 19, Sarah Good, Sarah Wildes, Elizabeth How, Susanna Martin and Rebecca Nurse; August 19, George Burroughs, John Procter, George Jacobs, sen., John Willard, and Martha Carrier; September 22, Martha Corey, Mary Easty, Alice Parker, Ann Pudeator, Margaret Scott, Wilmot Reed, Samuel Wardwell and Mary Parker; September 19, Giles Corey pressed to death.

The following were condemned but not executed : At the third session of the court in August, Elizabeth Procter; fourth session, Dorcas Hoar; fifth session, Abigail Faulkner, Rebecca Eames, Mary Lacy, Ann Foster and Abigail Hobbs; at the January session of the new court in 1693, Mary Post, Sarah Wardwell and Elizabeth Johnson.

Below will be found a partial list of persons accused whether convicted or not: Andover, Nehemiah Abbott, Sarah Bridges, Abigail Barker, William Barker, William Barker, jun., Mary Barker, John Bradstreet, Mrs. Ebenezer Baker, William Barry, Martha Carrier, Richard Carrier, Sarah Cave, Deliverance Dane, Mrs. Nathan Dane, Abigail Faulkner, Ann Foster, Eunice Frye, —— Harrington, Stephen Johnson, John Laundry, Mary Lacy, Mary Marston, Mary Osgood, Mary Parker, Hannah Tyler, Martha Tyler, Joanna Tyler, Hope Tyler, Samuel Wardwell, Sarah Wilson, Sarah Wilson, jun., Mary Wardwell.

Amesbury, Susanna Martin.

Beverly, Dorcas Hoar, Rebecca Johnson, Sarah Merrill, Sarah Morey, Susanna Roote, Sarah Riste, Job Tukey and John Wright.

Boxford, Rebecca Eames and Robert Eames.

Boston, John Alden and John Flood.

Billerica, Goodman Abbott, M. Andrews, Mary Toothaker, Jason Toothaker and Roger Toothaker.

Chelmsford, Martha Sparks.

Charlestown, Elizabeth Carey and Elizabeth Payne.

Gloucester, Mary Coffin, Ann Doliver, Martha Prince and Abigail Somes.

Haverhill, Mary Greene and Mrs. Francis Hutchinson.

Lynn, Sarah Bassett, Sarah Cole, Mary Derick, Mary Derrill, Thomas Farrar, Elizabeth Hart, Mary Ireson and Mary Rich.

Malden, Elizabeth Fosdick.

Marblehead, Wilmot Reed.

Reading, Elizabeth Colson, Sarah Dustin, Lydia Dustin and Sarah Rice.

Rowley, Mary Post and Margaret Scott.

Salem, Candy (an Indian slave), Phillip English, Mary English, Thomas Hardy, Alice Parker, Sarah Pease, Ann Pudeator, Mary de Riels and Mrs. White.

Salem Village and Farms, Daniel Andrews, Edward Bishop, Bridget Bishop, Sarah Bishop, Mary Black, John Buxton, Sarah Bibber, Sarah Buckley, Sarah Cloyse, Martha Corey, Giles Corey, Sarah Good, Dorothy Good, John Indian, George Jacobs, sen., George Jacobs, jun., Margaret Jacobs, Martha Jacobs, Rebecca Jacobs, Rebecca Nurse, John Procter, Elizabeth Procter, Benjamin Procter, William Procter, Tituba, Mary Warren, Mary Whittridge and John Willard.

Salisbury, Mary P. Bradbury.

Topsfield, Nehemiah Abbott, jun., Mary Easty, Abigail Hobbs, Deliverance Hobbs, William Hobbs, Elizabeth How, James How and Sarah Wildes.

Wells, Me., George Burroughs.

Woburn, Bethia Carter.

Residence unknown, Rachel Clinton.

Sarah Osburn and Ann Foster were convicted and sentenced, but died in prison.

APPENDIX B.

The question whether the attainders were ever removed
and whether the heirs of all the sufferers ever received
compensation at the hands of the General Court has been
ably and exhaustively argued by Mr. A. C. Goodell of
Salem, editor of the Province Laws, and Dr. George H.
Moore of New York, in papers read before the Massachusetts Historical Society and published in the proceedings of
that society, and also in pamphlet form. Both of these
authorities agreed that an act passed in 1703 reversing the
attainders of Abigail Faulkner, Sarah Wardwell and Elizabeth Procter. The records in the office of the clerk of
courts in Salem contain a statement of the amounts allowed
in the case of each person and also the acknowledgment
of the receipt of the money by numerous claimants. The
following document shows beyond question that pecuniary
compensation was made to many of the sufferers whether
the attaint was ever fully removed or not:

By His Excellency the Governor.

Whereas ye Generall Assembly in their last Session ac-
cepted ye report of their comitte appointed to consider of ye
Damages Sustained by Sundry persons prosecuted for
Witchcraft in ye year 1692 Viz^t.

To Elizabeth How	12-0-0	John Procter & wife	150-0-0
George Jacobs	79-0-0	Sarah Wild	14-0-0
Mary Easty	20-0-0	Mary Bradbury	20-0-0
Mary Parker	8-0-0	Abigail Faulkner	20-0-0
George Burroughs	50-0-0	Abigail Hobbs	10-0-0
Giles Corey & wife	21-0-0	Anne Foster	6-10-0
Rebeccah Nurse	25-0-0	Rebeccah Eames	10-0-0
John Willard	20-0-0	Dorcas Hoar	21-17-0
Sarah Good	30-0-0	Mary Post	8-14-0
Martha Carrier	7-6-0	Mary Lacey	8-10-0
Samuel Wardwell &			———
wife	36-15-0		
	———		269-11-00
	309-01-00		309-01-00
			———
			578-12-00

The whole amounting unto Five Hundred Seventy Eight poundes & Twelve Shillings.

I do by & with the advice & consent of Her Maj^{tey*} council hereby order you to pay ye above Sum of five hundred Seventy Eight poundes & Twelve shillings to Stephen Sewall Esqr. who together with ye Gentlemen of ye Comitte that Estimated and Reported ye Said Damages are desired & directed to distribute ye Same in proportion as above to such of ye Said persons as are Living & to those that legally represent them that are dead according as ye law directs for which this shall be your warrant.

Given under my hand at Boston
the 17 day of December 1711.
J: Dudley

To Mr. Treasurer Taylor
By order of ye Governor & Council
Is^a Addington Secr^ty

Other papers on the same files contain the receipts of the heirs of the above named parties for the amounts allowed to them. It will be seen that the names of six persons who were executed do not appear in this list, neither does that of Elizabeth Johnson jr. who was condemned but not executed, nor that of Sarah Osburn who died in prison. I do not find that their heirs ever received any compensation for the damages sustained by their persons and estates. Apparently none of the heirs of the six who were condemned ever petitioned for reimbursement or for the removal of the attaint. For this reason doubtless their names do not appear in the list reported upon by the committee. Elizabeth Johnson did sign the petition, but her name was omitted, either accidentally, or purposely because of her bad character.

APPENDIX C.

The letter of Gov. Phips to the home government under date of Feb. 21, 1692-3 is as follows:

May it please yor Lords^hp.

By the Capn. of ye Samuell & Henry I gave an account

that att my arrivall here I found ye Prisons full of people
comitted upon suspicion of witchcraft & that continuall
complaints were made to me that many persons were grievously tormented by witches & that they cryed out upon
severall persons by name, as ye cause of their torments ye
number of these complaints increasing every day, by advice of ye Lieut. Govr. & ye Councill I gave a Comission of
Oyer and Terminer to try ye suspected witches & *at that
time* the generality of ye People represented ye matter to
me as reall witchcraft & gave very strange instances of the
same.   The first in Comission was ye Lieut. Govr. & ye rest
persons of ye best prudence & figure that could then be
pitched upon & I depended upon ye Court for a right
method of proceeding in cases of witchcraft; at that time I
went to comand the army at ye Eastern part of the
Province for ye French and Indians had made an attack
upon some of our Frontier Towns, I continued there for
some time but *when I returned I found people much dissatisfied at ye proceedings of ye Court* for about Twenty persons were condemned and *executed* of which number *some*
were *thought by many persons to be innocent. The Court
still proceeded in ye same method of trying them*, which was
by ye evidence of ye afflicted persons who when they were
brought into ye Court as soon as the suspected witches
looked upon them instantly fell to ye ground in strange
agonies & grievous torments, but when touchd by them
upon ye arme or some other part of their flesh they imed-
iately revived & came to themselves, upon [which] they
made oath that ye Prisoner at ye Bar did afflict them &
that they saw their shape or spectre come from their bodies
which put them to such paines & torments: When I en-
quired into ye matter I was enformed by ye Judges that
they begun with this, but had humane testimony against
such as were condemned & undoubted proof of their being
witches, but at length I found that the Devill did take upon him ye shape of innocent persons & some were accused
of whose innocency I was well assured & *many considerable
persons* of unblameable life & conversation were cried out

upon as witches & wizards the *Deputy Govr.* notwithstand-ing *persisted vigorously in ye same method to ye great disat-isfaction & disturbance of ye people* untill I put an end to ye Court & stopped ye proceedings which I did because I saw many innocent persons might otherwise perish & at that time I thought it my duty to give an account thereof that their Ma^tes . pleasure might be signified hoping that for the better ordering thereof ye *judges learned in the law in England might give such rules & directions as have been practiced in England* for proceedings in so difficult & so nice a point; When I put an end to ye Court there were at least fifty persons in prison *in great misery by reason of the extreme cold & their poverty* most of them having only spec-tre evidence against them & their mittimusses being defec-tive I caused some of them to be lett out upon bayle & put ye judges upon considering of a way to reliefe others & *prevent them from perishing in prison, upon which some of them were convinced & acknowledged that their former pro-ceedings were too violent & not grounded upon a right foun-dation but that if they might sit againe they would proceed after another method* & whereas Mr. Increase Mather & severall other Divines did give it as their Judgement that ye Devill might afflict in ye shape of an innocent person & that ye look & ye touch of ye suspected persons was not sufficient proofe against them, these things had not ye same stress layd upon them as before & upon this consideration I permitted a speciall Superior Court to be held at Salem in ye County of Essex on ye third day of January ye Lieut. Govr. being Chief Judge their method of proceeding being altered, all that were brought to tryall to ye number of fifety two, were cleared saving three & *I was enformed by the Kings Attorny Generall that some of ye cleared and ye condemned were under ye same circumstances* or that there was ye same reason to clear ye three condemned as ye rest according to his Judgement. The Deputy Govr. signed a Warrant for their execution & also of five others who were condemned at ye former Court of Oyer and terminer but considering how ye matter had been managed I sent a re-priev whereby ye execution was stopped until their Maj.

pleasure be signified & declared *the Lieut. Gov. upon this occasion was inraged & filled with passionate anger & refused to sitt on ye bench in a Superior Court then held* [*Tuesday, January* 31, 1693] *at Charles Towne & indeed hath from the begining hurried on these matters with great precipitancy & by his warrant hath caused the estates, goods and chattles of ye executed to be seized & disposed of without my knowledge or consent, the stop put to ye first method* of proceedings hath dissipated ye blak cloud that threatened this Province with destruccon; for whereas this delusion of ye Devill did spread & its dismall effects touched ye lives & estates of many of their Ma^tes. Subjects & ye reputacon of *some of ye principall persons here* & indeed unhappily clogged and interrupted their Mates. affaires which hath been a great vexation to me! I have no new complaints but *peoples minds before divided and distracted by differing opinions* concerning this matter are now well composed.

I am Yor. Lordships most faithfull humble Servant,

William Phips.

To the Rt. Honble. the Earle of Nottingham, att Whitehall, London.

APPENDIX D.

The most noted of the English cases of witchcraft, and the one most frequently cited in the Salem trials, was that heard before Lord Chief Justice Hale in Bury St. Edmunds in 1665. On that occasion Amy Duny and Rose Cullender were the accused and were tried together. The report of this celebrated trial is found in volume 6, "State Trials," page 647, and from that report the following account has been condensed.

The morning the afflicted came into the hall to give instructions for the drawing of their bills of indictment, three of them fell into strange and violent fits, shrieking out in a most sad manner, so that they could not in any wise give any instruction in the court who were the cause of their distemper. And although they did after some certain space recover out of their fits, yet they were every one of them struck dumb, so that none of them could speak neither at that time, nor during the assizes until the conviction of the supposed witches. Elizabeth Pacy, eleven years of age, one of the afflicted, was brought into court at the time of the framing of the indictment and afterwards at the trial of the prisoners, but could not speak one word all the time, and for the most part she remained as one wholly senseless, as one in a deep sleep, and could move no part of her body, and all the motion of life that appeared in her was, that as she lay upon cushions in the court upon her back, her stomache and belly, by the drawing of her breath, would arise to a great height; and after the said Elizabeth had lain a long time on the table in the court, she came to a little herself and sat up, but could neither see nor speak, but was sensible of what was said to her, and after a while she laid her head on the bar of the court with a cushion under it, and her hand and her apron upon that, and there she lay a good space of time: and by the direction of the judge Amy Duny was privately brought to Elizabeth Pacy, and she touched her hand; whereupon the child without so much as seeing her for her eyes were closed all the while, suddenly leaped up, and catched Amy Duny by the hand, and afterwards by the face; and with her nails scratched her till the blood came and would by no means leave her till she was taken from her.

Deborah was held in such extreme agony that her parents wholly dispaired of her life, and therefore could not bring her to the assizes. Samuel Pacy, the father, testified that Deborah was suddenly taken with lameness in one leg. The same day Amy Duny came to the house to buy some herrings. She came three times and was denied three times, and the last time went away grumbling. At the same instant Deborah was taken with violent fits, feeling most extreme pain in her stomache, like the pricking of pins, and shrieking out in a most dreadful manner like unto

262

APPENDIX.

a whelp. She continued in this extremity from Oct. 10 to the 30th of the same month. The child cried out against Amy Duny as the cause of her malady. Soon the other child was taken, then both cried out, " There stands Amy Duny, and the Rose Cullender." They continued thus for two months. The father in the intervals caused them to read in the New Testament, and when they would come to the name of Lord, or Jesus, or Christ, and then before they could pronounce either of said words they would suddenly fall into their fits. But when they would come to the name Satan, or devil, they would clap their fingers upon the book, crying out, " This bites but makes me speak quite well."

Margaret Arnold, Pacy's sister, testified that her brother brought the children to her as she lived in Yarmouth She did not believe the children vomited pins but that they were playing tricks, so she took all the pins out of their clothes and sewed them on, yet they afterwards raised at several times at least 30 pins in her presence. At times the young child went to the door when something which looked like a bee flew at her mouth. She ran into the house and fell into a fit, vomiting up a two-penny nail with a broad head. The child said the bee brought the nail and forced it into her mouth. The elder child at times declared that flies came to her and brought pins and afterwards she raised several pins.

Dianna Becking deposed, that her daughter had fits and she was taken with pains in her stomache, like pricking with pins; and afterwards fell into swooning fits, taking little or no food and daily vomiting crooked pins, " and upon Sunday last raised seven pins." These pins and also a lathe nail were produced in court. Mary Chandler, mother of Susan Chandler, another of the afflicted, testified to searching the body of Rose Cullender and finding various excrescenses of flesh and other things not proper to mention here. She also testified that her daughter had terrible fits and vomited up crooked pins, all of which mother and daughter attributed to Rose Cullender. The girl was immediately brought into court and immediately struck dumb, crying out, " burn her," " burn her."

At the hearing, continues the report, there were divers
known persons as Mr. Serjeant Kneeling, Mr. Serjeant
Earl, and Mr. Serjeant Barnard present. Serjeant Kneeling
seemed dissatisfied with the evidence; and thought it not
sufficient to convict the prisoners: for admitting that the
children were in truth bewitched, yet, said he, it can never
be applied to the prisoners, upon the imagination only of
the parties afflicted; for if that might be allowed, no person whatsoever can be in safety, for perhaps they might
fancy another person, who might altogether be innocent in
such matters. Dr. Brown of Norwich, " a person of great
knowledge, who after this evidence given and upon view of
the three persons in court, was desired to give his opinion,
what he did concieve of them; and he was clearly of opinion that the persons were bewitched: and said that in Den-
mark there had been lately a great discovery of witches,
who used the very same way of afflicting persons, by conveying pins into them, and crooked as these pins were, with
needles and nails. And his opinion was that the devil in
such cases did work upon the bodies of men and women,
upon a natural foundation (that is) to stir up, and excite
such super-abounding in their bodies to a great excess
whereby he did in an extraordinary manner afflict them
with such distempers as their bodies were most subject to
as particularly appeared in these children, for he conceived
that these swooning fits were natural, and nothing else but
that they call the mother, but only heightened to a great
excess by the subtilty of the devil, cooperating with the
malice of these which we term witches, at whose instance
he doth these villainies."
At first during the trial, there were some experiments
made with the persons afflicted by bringing the persons to
touch them; and it was observed, that when they were in
the midst of their fits, to all men's apprehension wholly
deprived of all sense and understanding, closing their fists
in such manner, as that the strongest man in court could
not force them open; yet by the least touch of one of these
supposed witches, Rose Cullender by name, they would
suddenly shriek out opening their hands, which accident

would not happen by the touch of any other person. There was what the report calls, "an ingenious person," who thought there might be great fallacy in the experiment and that the children might counterfeit their distemper. Thereupon Lord Conwallis, Sir Edmund Bacon and Mr. Serjeant Kneeling retired to the further end of the hall while one of the distempered was here in her fits. Amy Duny was conveyed from the bar and brought to the maid; they put an apron before her eyes, and then another person touched her hand, which produced the same effect as the touch of the witch did in court. Whereupon the gentlemen returned, openly protesting, that they did believe the whole transaction of this business was a mere imposture.[1]

This put the court and all persons into a stand. But at length Mr. Pacy declared that possibly the maid might be deceived by a suspicion that the witch touched her when she did not. When his daughter recovered she confirmed this and said that while she had been unable to speak, she heard and understood all that was going on in the court. This was looked upon as a confirmation of the experiment and that the parties were bewitched. It being demanded of the prisoners what they had to say for themselves, they replied, nothing material to anything that was proved against them. Whereupon, continues the account, the judge in giving his direction to the jury told them, that he would not repeat the evidence unto them, lest by so doing he should wrong the evidence on the one side or the other. Only this acquainted them, that they had two things to enquire after. First, whether or no these children were bewitched? Secondly, whether or no the prisoners at the bar were guilty of it? That there were such creatures as witches he made no doubt at all; For first, the scriptures had affirmed so much. Secondly, the wisdom of all nations had provided laws against such persons, which is an argument of their confidence of such crime. And such hath been the judgment of this kingdom, as appears by that act of parliament which hath provided punishments propor-

1 It will be remembered that in the trials in Salem the touch of the witch on the afflicted restored them to their senses.

tionable to the quality of the offence. And desired them, strictly to observe their evidence; and desired the great God of heaven to direct their hearts in this weighty thing they had in hand: For to condemn the innocent, and to let the guilty go free, were both an abomination to the Lord.

With this short direction the jury retired and within half an hour returned with a verdict of guilty on the thirteen indictments. This was upon Thursday afternoon, March 13, 1665. The next morning the three children with their parents came to the Lord Chief Baron Hale's lodgings, who all of them spake perfectly, and were in as good health as ever they were. Mr. Pacy declared that they were all recovered within a half hour after the witches were convicted.

In conclusion the judge and all the court were fully satisfied with the verdict, and therefore gave judgement against the witches that they should be hanged. They were much urged to confess, but would not. That morning we departed for Cambridge, but no reprieve was granted; and they were executed on Monday the 17th of March following, but they confessed nothing.

In 1716, almost a quarter of a century after the last witch was hung in New England, a Mrs. Hicks and her daughter aged nine years were hanged in Huntingdon for selling their souls to the devil, tormenting and destroying the neighbors and causing them to vomit pins, and raising a storm so that ships were almost lost by pulling off her stockings and making a lather with soap. Arnot says the last execution for witchcraft in Scotland was in 1722, when a woman was brought to the stake. Other writers say that the last execution in the south of Scotland was in 1696, when, among others, a handsome young woman suffered; and the last instance in the north of Scotland was in 1729. The statute against witchcraft was repealed in England by 9th Geo., 2, in 1736.

Index.

Abbey, Samuel 55.
Abbott, Benj. 185, 255.
" Nehemiah, 223-4, 244, 254.
" N., jr, 255.
Addington, Isaac, 170, 257.
Alden, John, 230-1, 255.
Alford, Wm., 20.
Allen, Rev. James, 113, 176.
Amesbury, 190, 254.
Andover, 87, 91, 205, 254.
Andrews, D. 255.
Andrews, M., 255.
Andros, Sir Edmund, 20, 28, 70.
Antimonian Views, 19.
Appleton, Samuel, 170.
Arnold, Margaret, 262.
Bacon, Sir Edmund, 264.
Ballard, Joseph 205, Mrs.206.
Bailey, John 173.
Bailey, Rev. Mr., 176.
Barnard, Rev. Thomas, 206.
Barry, Wm., 254.
Bassett, Sarah, 255.
Batchelder, Jno., 62.
Batten, Wm., 61.
Battis, Wm., 63.
Bayley, Rev. James, 131.
Beach, Rev., 35.
Beadle Tavern, 74, 160, 180, 194, 197.
Becking, Hannah, 262.
Bellingham, Dept. Gov., 36.
Benom, Mrs., 89.
Bently, Dr. Wm., 216.
Best, John, sen., 199, jr. 199.
Beverly, 15, 222, 254.

Bibber, Sarah, 204, 255.
Billerica 255.
Bishop, Bridget, 72, 77, 80, 148-158, 226, 254, 255.
" Edward, 148, 255.
" Hannah, 148.
" Sarah, 255.
" Townsend, 20, 111.
Black, Mary, 255.
Blackstone, 25, 26, 106.
Bly, John, 155.
Bodily presence, 105, 218.
Boston, 16, 43, 44, 87, 255,
" jail, 60, 67, 68.
Book, the devil's, 27, 61, 202
Booth, Eliz., 172, 200, 244.
Boxford, 198, 207, 255.
Bradstreet, Dudley and wife 206.
" John (Andover), 206, 254.
" John (of Rowley), 34.
" Simon, Gov., 41, 236.
Bradbury, Mary Perkins, 85, 210-14, 255.
Bridges, Sarah, 254.
Broomsticks, 27, 61.
Brown, Dr., 263.
Browne, John and Samuel, 14, 19.
Brown, Sir Thomas, 24.
Buckley, Sarah, 179, 232, 233, 254, 255.
Buffum, Caleb, 77.
Buffinton, Thos., 63.
Bullock, Jno., 198.
Burial of witches, 77.

Burroughs, Rev. Geo., 48, 61, 80, 84. 131-147, 165, 199, 218, 240, 243, 254-6.

Burroughs, Mrs. Geo., 134.

Buxton, John, 204, 255.

Calef, Rob't, quoted from, 43, 48, 54, 68, 95, 107, 156, 240.

Cambridge, 230.

Candy, 255.

Cape Ann, 10.

Carey, Jonathan and wife, 227, 230, 254-5.

Carr, George, 211.
" James, 211.
" Mary, 132.
" Richard, 212, 244.
" William, 213.

Carrier, Andrew, 185.
" Martha, 85, 146, 182, 184-6, 205, 254-6.
" Richard, 185.
" Sarah, 185.

Carter, Bethia, 255.

Casco, Me., 134.

Cats, 27, 68, 185.

Cave, Sarah, 254.

Charlestown, 15, 44, 87, 255.

Charter, 70.

Charter Street Cemetery, 41.

Cheever, Ezekiel, 57, 98, 147.
" Samuel, 233.

Chekley, Anthony, 73.

Chelmsford, 256.

Chickering, Henry, 111.

Chilburn, Johanna, 61.

Children in witchcraft, 46, 209, 243.

Churchill, Sarah, 46, 160-2.

Church of England, 9, 10.

Cleeves. William, 108.

Clinton, Rachel, 255.

Cloyse, Sarah, 169, 171, 193, 194, 195, 196, 255.

Coffin, Mary, 255.

Cole, Ann, 36, 37. Sarah, 255

Colson, Eliz., 255.

Commissioners of Oyer and Terminer, 70.

Conant, Roger, 10, 19.

Conwallis, Lord, 264.

Cook, John, 156.

Corey, Giles, 89, 97-110, 144, 168, 254-6.
" Martha, 85, 97-110, 225, 244, 254-5.

Corwin, George, 73.
" Jonathan, 16, 53, 72, 74, 101, 170, 198, 228, 231.

Court.
Assistants, 246.
Established in 1692, 86.
General, 33, 35, 70, 82, 86, 114, 115, 132, 248, 256.
Oyer and Terminer, 77-87, 91, 92-4, 150, 246, 258-9.
Sessions in 1693, 87.
Special assizes, 86, 236.
" or Superior, 91, 259.

Crowninshield, B. W., 193.

Cullender, Rose, 260-5.

Dane, Deliverance, 206, 254.
" Rev. Francis, 206.
" Nathan, 254.

Danforth, 87, 170.

Danvers, 15.

Delius, Godfrey, 95.

Demonology, 22.

Derich, John, 105.

Derick, Mary, 255.

Derrill, Mary, 255.

Dodd, Sarah, 203.

Dog bewitched, 206.

Dolliver, Ann, 255.

Drake, 69.

Dudley, Joseph, 72, 257.

Dudley, of N. Y., 95.

Duny, Amy, 260-5.

Dustin, Good, 61. Sarah and Lydia, 255.

Eames, Rebecca, 28, 85, 231, 254-6.
" Robert, 231, 255.

Eastey, Isaac, 116, 193.
" Mary, 85, 116, 193-6, 254-6.

Elliott, Daniel, 174.

Endicott, C. M. 164.
" John, 10, 15, 16, 19, 35, 111, 236, John jr., 113.

INDEX.

Endicott, Samuel, 213,
" Zerubabel, 114, 172,
212, 232.
England, 70-72.
English, Phillip and Mary,
216-17, 255.
" Phillip's house, 215.
" precedents, 73, 239,
247, 260-5.
Essex County, 38, 87, 249.
Evidence, spectral, 92, 105,
230, 236, 238, 241, 247.
Fairfax, Edward, 24.
Falmouth, Me., 143.
Fast Day, 44, 49, 248, 251.
Faulkner, Abagail, 85, 206,
254-6.
Felton, Nathaniel, 175.
First Church, Boston, 113.
" " Salem, 12, 13,
19, 74, 128, 233, 249.
" Church, Salem, cove-
nant of, 13.
Fiske, Thomas, 128.
Foster, Ann, 85, 89, 206, 254-6
" Constable, 208.
Freemen, 91.
Fuller, Benjamin, 181.
" John, 172.
" Thomas, 179, 183.
Gadge, Sarah, 55-6.
Gallows Hill, 41,76-7,146,231.
Gardner, Captain, 107.
Gedney, Bartholomew, 72,
198, 231.
Gloucester, 255.
Glover, Mrs. Mary, 43, 72.
Gloyd, John, 168.
Godfrey, John, 36.
Good, Dorcas, 64, 255.
" Sarah, 50-2-3, 54-60, 65,
84, 144, 254-6.
" William, 54.
Goodell, A. C., 74, 256.
" Jacob, 109.
Goodwin family, 43, 242.
Gray, Samuel, 149.
" William, 20.
Green, Rev. Joseph, 250.
Green, Mary, 255.
Greenslit, Thomas, 142, 199.

Greensmiths, The, 36.
Griggs, Dr., 46, 48.
Groton, Mass., 37.
Haines, Thomas, house, 201.
Hale, Rev. John, 18, 39, 41,
147, 152, 229, 243, 248.
" Mrs., 90.
" Sir Matthew, 24, 260-5.
Harrington, 254.
Hathorne, John, 16, 53, 59,
72, 100, 101, 170, 194,
198, 221, 222, 228, 229,
231.
Harvard College, 16, 132.
Harwood, John, 121.
Haverhill, 255.
Herrick, Marshal George, 73,
116, 162, 204, 210.
" Henry, 62.
Hibbins, Ann, 34-5.
Higginson, Rev. Francis, 11,
12, 15.
" John, 198.
" Rev. John, 233.
Hoar, Dorcas, 85, 222-3, 254,
256.
Hobbs, Abagail, 61, 85, 105,
144, 217-22, 254-6.
" Deliverance, 61, 144,
217-22, 255.
" William, 204, 217-22,
255.
Holland, 12.
Holt, Ch. J., 24.
Holten, Benj., Sarah, 121,
122.
Holyoke, Rev. Dr., 76.
House of deputies, 41.
Howe, Elizabeth, 84, 186-9,
254-6.
" James, 186, 188, 255.
" Capt. John, 188.
Hubbard, Elizabeth, 46, 57,
60, 62-3, 119-20-21, 139,
150, 200, 202, 222, 244.
Hutchinson, Ann, 19.
" Benjamin, 143,
194, 233.
" Elisha, 137.
" Gov. quoted
from 30, 43, 79, 80, 85.

Hutchinson, John, 150.
" Joseph, 53.
Indian, John, 49, 169, 170, 191, 202, 255.
Ingersoll, Lieut. Nathaniel, 53, 116, 169.
" Sarah, 162.
Ingersoll's Tavern, 74, 182, 200, 222.
Intolerance of Puritans, 19.
Ipswich, 34, 40, 54, 67, 87, 115, 233.
Jacobs family, 158-67, 255.
Jacobs, George, Sr., 48, 85, 146, 254, 256.
Jailors' fees, 234.
Jails,
Boston, 223, 230.
Ipswich, 54, 67, 223.
Salem, 74.
Jones, Margaret, 31-2.
Johnson, Elizabeth, Jr., 87, 206, 207, 254, 257.
" Sarah, 207.
" Stephen, 254.
Juries, 91, 236, 249.
Jury, grand, 80-82.
Kenney, Henry, 117.
Kemble, John, 192.
Knapp, Elizabeth, 37.
Kneeling, Serg't, 263-4.
Knife blade, 64.
Lacey, Mary, 85, 207, 254-6.
Lane, Francis, 188.
Lander, John, 154.
Laundry, John, 254.
Lawrence, Mary, 218.
Lawson, Rev. Deodat, 133, 178.
Lawyers, 73.
Lewis, John, 150.
" Mercy, 46, 48, 63, 65, 139, 140, 141, 150, 169, 170, 172, 179, 194, 200, 202, 221, 224, 244.
Locker, Constable George, 57.
Lord's Prayer, 146, 228, 240.
Lyford, John, 10.
Lynn, 177, 255.
Malden, 255.

Manchester, 15.
Marblehead, 15, 199, 255.
Marshfield, Widow, 33.
Marston, Mary, 254.
Martin, Susannah, 84, 190-93, 254.
Massachusetts Bay, 10.
Mather, Cotton, 16, 43, 72, 82, 87, 95, 135, 136, 146, 239-43.
Mather, Increase, 16, 35, 36, 135, 176, 240, 259.
Maverick, Widow, 211.
Merrill, Sarah, 254.
Middleton, 15, 115.
Ministers, their answer, 82.
' Dutch, 95.
" of Essex County, 249
Moody, Lady Deborah, 20.
" Rev. 176.
Moore, Geo. H., 256.
More, Dr. 24.
Morey, Sarah, 254.
Morse, William, 38, 40.
Morse, Mrs., 41.
Moulton, John, 108.
Moxon children, 33.
Nantasket, 10.
Naumkeag, 10.
Neal, Jos., 159.
Nelson, Phillip, 203.
Newbury, 38, 41, 115, 191.
Newburyport, 38.
New England, 10, 236.
Newton, Thomas, 73, 80.
Nichols, Elizabeth, 219.
" John, 221.
" Lydia, 219.
North Beverly, 148.
Northend, 92.
Norton, John, 35.
Nottingham, Earl of, 259.
Noyes, N. Rev., 16, 18, 65, 85, 101, 147, 162, 243.
Nurse family, 113.
" Francis, 111.
" Rebecca, 79, 84, 111-130, 150, 169, 193, 238, 254.
" Samuel, 116.
Oliver, Thos., 148.
Osburn, Alex., 65.

INDEX.

Osburn, Sarah, 50, 52, 53, 59, 61, 65-68, 89, 255, 257.
Osgood, Mary, 206, 254.
Pacy, Eliz. and Samuel, 261.
Parris, Eliz., 46, 51, 56, 62-3, 119, 236.
" Rev. Samuel, 16, 18, 25, 46, 48, 49, 50, 57, 101, 103, 117, 134, 171, 224, 225, 227, 237, 238, 243.
Parker, Alice, 196, 254, 255.
" John, 196.
" Mary, 85, 196, 198, 205, 254, 256.
Parsons, Mary, 33.
" Hugh, 33.
Partridge, Jno., 137.
Payne, Elizabeth, 255.
Payson, Rev. 189.
Peabody. town, 15.
Peach, Barnard, 192.
Pease, Sarah, 255.
Peirce, T. W., 193.
Perkins, Wm., 25.
Perley, Deborah, 187.
" John, 188.
" Timothy, 187.
Phillips, Sam'l, 189.
Phips, Sir Wm., 20, 29, 41, 70, 71, 73, 87, 92-6, 150, 177, 207, 242, 257.
Pietrus, Peter, 95.
Pickworth, Sam'l 199.
Pins, witch, 49, 63, 231, 262.
Pitman, Charity, 203.
Plymouth, 10, 12.
Pope, Mrs. 103.
Poppits, 153.
Portland, Me., 132.
Post, Mary, 87, 254, 256.
Powell, Caleb, 39, 40.
Preston, Rebecca, 124.
" Thomas, 53, 116, 238.
Prince, Robert, 65.
Prime, Martha, 255.
Proclamation, freedom, 87-94.
Procter Benj. and Wm., 255.
Procter, Eliz., 85, 168, 177, 254-6.

Procter, John, 84, 105, 110, 146, 168-177, 225, 243, 254, 256.
Protests, against trials, 91.
Pudeator, Ann, 85, 196, 198-9 254, 255.
" Jacob, 198.
Puritans, 9.
Putnam, Allen, 37, 54.
" Ann, 46, 57, 60, 62, 63, 65, 98, 100, 108, 109, 116, 117, 120, 139, 140, 141, 145, 150, 169, 170, 190, 194, 202, 205, 224, 236, 244, 246, 250.
" Mrs. Ann, 116, 117, 122, 180-2, 211, 213, 244, 246.
" Edward, 53, 98, 100, 116, 122, 238.
" John, 115, 133, 179, 194, 205.
" John 3rd, 220.
" Joseph, 236.
" Nathaniel, 103, 114, 132, 159.
" Serg't Thos., 46, 53, 68, 108, 116, 117, 132, 133, 141, 204, 211, 238, 246.
Putnams, The, 16.
Reading, 255.
Reed, Saml., 199.
Reed, Wilmot, 85, 196, 199-203, 254, 255.
Reimbursed heirs, 248, 256.
Repentance of accusers, etc., 248-255.
Rice, Rev. C. B., 23.
Rice, Sarah, 255.
Rich, Mary, 255.
Richards, John, 72, 87, 136, 241.
Riels, Mary de, 255.
Riste, Sarah, 254.
Roote, Susannah, 254.
Rowley, 34, 87, 203, 255.
Rule, Margaret, 87-88.
Saco, Me., 143.
Salem, 9, 12, 14, 15, 16, 41, 44, 87, 89, 115, 216, 236, 255.

Salem Village, 43, 45, 46, 52, 53, 74, 115, 131, 133, 173, 204, 236, 255.
Salem Village Church, 131.
Salisbury, 210, 255.
Saltonstall, Nathaniel, 72.
" Richard, 15.
Sargent, Peter, 72.
Scott, Margaret, 85, 196, 203, 254, 255.
Scottow, John, 35.
Sewall, Judge Sam., 72, 87, 108, 110, 138, 170, 223, 241, 251.
" Stephen, 79, 257.
Selpins, Henry, 95.
Shapling, L., 172.
Shattuck, Sam., 154, 198, 245.
Shaw, Deborah, 61.
Shaw, Elizabeth, 172.
" William, 61.
Sheldon, Johanna, 122.
Sheldon, Samuel, 145, 245.
" Susan, 61, 62, 139, 182, 184, 202, 244.
Shepard, Rebecca, 121.
Sherwood, Grace, 45.
Shilleto, Robert, 203.
Sims, Rev. Mr., 147.
Sibley, Sam., 62.
Skelton, Rev. Sam., 11, 12, 15.
Small, Thos., 65.
Smith, Jas., 200.
Somes. Abagail, 255.
South Carolina, 45.
Sparks, Martha, 255.
Sprague, Martha, 198, 207.

Spiritualism, 22.
Springfield, 33.
Stacey, William, 151.
Stiles, John, 38.
Stone, Robt. Sr., Robt. Jr., 172, 173.
Stoughton, Wm., 71, 87, 92, 93, 138, 247-8, 259, 260.
Swan, Tim., 185.
Symonds, John, 76.
Syms, Mrs., 203.
Tarbell, John, Mary, 123, 124.
Tavern, Beadle's, 160, 180.
" Ingersoll's, 53.
Taylor, Treas., 257.
Tituba, 46, 49, 51, 52, 53, 60, 68-9, 119, 223, 255.
Toothaker, Jason, Mary, Roger, 255.
Topsfield, 15, 193, 204.
" controversy, 114-16, 255.
Tortures, 176.
Townes, John J. Jr., 115-16.
" Jos., 221.
Trask, Christian, John, 152-3.
Trials by Jury, 77-87, 136.
" preliminary, 74-246.
Tukey, Job, 254.
Tyler, Hannah, Hope, Johanna, Martha, 254.
Upham, C. W. 54
Varich, Rudolph, 95.
Vibber, Sarah, John, 60, 62, 63, 121.
Virginia, 45.